Signs and Wonders

D1477808

Signs and Wonders

Dr. Norman Geisler

Tyndale House
Publishers, Inc.
Wheaton, Illinois

Scripture quotations, unless otherwise noted, are
taken from *The Holy Bible,* New International
Version. Copyright 1973, 1978, 1984 International
Bible Society. Used by permission of Zondervan
Bible Publishers.

Scripture quotations marked NASB are from the
New American Standard Bible. Copyright 1960,
1962, 1963, 1971, 1973 by The Lockman
Foundation.

Library of Congress Catalog Card Number 88-71948
ISNB 0-8423-5904-4
Copyright 1988 by Norman L. Geisler
Printed in the United States of America
2   3   4   5   6   7   8   9   10   95   94   93   92   91   90   89

To my wife, Barbara, who in a labor of love has typed and greatly improved many thousands of manuscript pages for me over the past thirty years. Greater love has no author's wife than this.

Contents

Acknowledgments

I wish to thank Robert Anderson, Warren Culwell, Karl Elkins, David Geisler, David Gowdey, Tom Howe, and Craig Schilling for their help in refining the ideas expressed in this book. Their insightful questions and interaction, as well as their zeal to know the truth about signs and wonders, was an inspiration to complete this project. I am grateful for all their efforts.

I also wish to express appreciation to Walter Martin, Thomas Edgar, and Roy Zuck for reading the manuscript and providing many helpful suggestions. Of course, I take full responsibility for the ideas expressed here. But due to their insights the final product is significantly improved.

1. Alice in Signs-and-Wonders-Land

The Christian in a World of Amazing Things

She ate a little bit, and said anxiously to herself "Which way? Which way?" holding her hand on the top of her head to feel which way it was growing, and she was quite surprised to find that she remained the same size: to be sure, this is what generally happens when one eats cake; but Alice had got so much into the way of expecting nothing but out-of-the-way things to happen, that it seemed quite dull and stupid for life to go on in the common way.

So amazed was Alice with her adventures in Wonderland that she "said nothing: she had sat down again with her face in her hands, wondering if anything would ever happen in a natural way again."

Today's Christian is like an Alice in modern "signs and wonders" land. Many wonderful things—healings, raisings from the dead—are being ascribed to the miraculous workings of God in our midst. Consider the words of pastor John Wimber, a leader in the current "signs and wonders" movement, about his healing ministry:

Today we see hundreds of people healed every month in Vineyard Christian Fellowship services. Many more are healed as we pray for them in hospitals, on the streets, and in homes. The blind see; the lame walk; the deaf hear. Cancer is disappearing. (Wimber 1986, 44)

What is the contemporary Christian to make of such things? Should we just praise the Lord and be thankful, or should we perhaps exercise a healthy skepticism?

Signs and Wonders—Are They Freaks of Nature?

In recent years there has been a great resurgence of interest in the supernatural. We have only to turn on the television to see a veritable smorgasbord of the "miraculous." Signs and wonders are performed in the local church, by the neighborhood psychic, perhaps even by your next-door neighbor. Odd events which seem to defy natural explanation are presented in newspapers, on talk shows, and in television miniseries. Are all of these things miracles? Are they from God? Is there a scientific explanation for such signs and wonders?

Scientists have observed and researched accounts of many events for which there seem to be no known natural explanation. Many have eventually been explained. Others, scientists optimistically promise us, will yet be explained; "we just haven't found it yet." The wonders that continue to elude scientific explanation are called anomalies. An anomaly is an odd event that seems to deviate from the normal way that nature operates. It is not necessarily a miracle, only a deviation from the normal.

It is a popular practice among skeptics (and even some who call themselves Christians) to question the authenticity of the miracles recorded in the Bible. Some classify the supernatural events in the Bible as mere anomalies, although most unbelievers go further and question the accuracy of the record.

Such skepticism may not always be such a bad thing. Indeed, some believe the Bible itself states that there are natural causes for certain so-called miraculous events.

Exodus 14 tells of the crossing of the Red Sea by the Israelites as they were departing from Egypt. As the armies of Pharaoh closed in on the helpless Israelites at the edge of the sea, the people became fearful and cried out to Moses. Moses told them to "Stand by and see the salvation of the Lord which He will accomplish for you today" (Exodus 14:13, NASB).

The Bible says that Moses stretched out his hand over the sea, "and the LORD swept the sea back by a strong east wind all night, and turned the sea into dry land, so the waters were divided" (Exodus 14:21, NASB). Was it God who parted the waters (using the wind as His agent), or was it merely the strong east wind (which the Israelites attributed to God)? Was this really a miracle, or was it merely an odd event that simply escapes scientific explanation and was later given a religious interpretation?

One natural explanation of the parting of the Red Sea was offered by Immanuel Velikovsky in 1950 in his book *Worlds in Collision*. He proposed the idea that "the planet Jupiter disgorged a large comet that made a grazing collision with Earth around 1500 B.C." (Abell 1981, 230). Velikovsky claimed that the interaction of the comet, its tail, and earth's atmosphere accounted for the various plagues recorded in the Book of Exodus. This occurred "at the moment that Moses lifts his rod and stretches out his hand, the Red Sea parts—either due to the gravitational tidal field of the comet or to some unspecified electrical or magnetic interaction between the comet and the Red Sea" (Abell 1981, 230). Were the events recorded in Exodus merely odd natural events, or were they supernatural acts of God?

The Bible is not the only place that records extraordinary events that defy natural explanation. One such event is reported to have occurred on May 26, 1907, in the small French town of Remiremont. It is reported that "during a hailstorm that struck at five-thirty that evening, several stones fell to the earth imprinted with the likeness of the Blessed Virgin Mary" (Rogo 1983, 141). According to another report, the devastation of an earthquake and its aftershocks were immediately stilled when the villagers marched through the town carrying a cedar wood statue of the Virgin Mary, which had become the property of the town. Thereafter the town vowed to reenact the procession each year to commemorate the event.

By 1907 the statue had still not received the official recognition by the pope. Finally, Pope Pius X sent a delegation to recognize the statue officially. A celebration was scheduled for May 20, 1907, which was to include a public procession.

However, on May 12 the town council refused to allow the procession due to a vocal anti-Catholic minority group. This decision caused a great controversy in the town. Nevertheless, May 20 passed without the annual public procession.

On the afternoon of May 26 the hailstorm struck. At first the day was clear, but late that afternoon the storm had moved in and the hail began to fall. According to the report, the first stones were small, but soon stones as big as tomatoes were falling. "Many of them were oval in shape and had a flattened (as opposed to a convex) side. These larger stones fell from roughly 5:30 to 6:15. A number of them were subsequently collected by curious villagers, who made a fascinating discovery. The stones were impressed with a portrait of the Virgin Mary!" (Rogo 1983, 144).

However, this is not the end of the story. In anticipation of the celebration the town had designed and made a commemorative medallion with the image of the Virgin Mary and the Christ child. "The image on the miraculous hailstones was, according to several witnesses, identical to that on the medallion!" (Rogo 1983, 144).

Was this a miracle, or merely a natural phenomenon that defies scientific explanation? One investigator of this event believed that "the hailstones were created by a divine intelligence as a 'sign' to those who had been robbed of their procession" (Rogo 1983, 151). Another held that "Somehow the collective 'will' of the townspeople acted directly on the weather and psychically produced the miraculous hailstones" (Rogo 1983, 152). Was it a miracle, magic, or an unexplained mystery?

The confusion about signs and wonders is increased by a multitude of claims of the supernatural by people all over the globe. Many of these claims have been debunked, but many are called fakery simply because there seem to be no scientific explanations.

Resurrection from the Dead—Fake or Fact?

Christians believe that when Jesus walked on this earth He performed many signs and wonders. One of the most significant was when He raised Lazarus from the dead. The Gospel of John says Lazarus became very ill, so that Jesus was called to come to Bethany in order to heal him before he died. However, when Jesus arrived, Lazarus had been dead and buried for four days. Both Mary and her sister Martha were disappointed that Jesus had not arrived in time to prevent Lazarus's death. Yet Jesus told them that if they would only believe they would "see the glory of God" (John 11:40, NASB).

Jesus came to the tomb of Lazarus and commanded that the stone be rolled away. Martha objected to this because after four days in the grave there would be a stench from the body. Nevertheless, the stone was rolled away. After Jesus gave thanks to the Father, "He cried out with a loud voice, 'Lazarus, come forth'" (John 11:43, NASB). According to the story, Lazarus immediately came forth from the grave, still bound hand and foot by the grave clothes.

This section of Scripture goes to great lengths to emphasize that Lazarus was truly dead. Several witnesses are quoted who state that he was dead. The passage points out that he had been in the tomb four days (John 11:39). However, the skeptic remains a skeptic.

Was this actually a demonstration of the power of God, or was it a setup? Was this simply a show that had been staged by some of Jesus' friends? Was Jesus' use of the phrase "Lazarus! Come forth!" a prearranged signal for the young man hiding in the tomb to emerge to the amazement of all? Or was this truly a miracle? Many would see no basis for such questions. To them the answers are quite obvious. But, if they are so obvious in the Gospels, what about the claims of some modern evangelists who say they have raised the dead?

A Modern Story of Resurrection. In the early 1960s a report was made in *Christian Life* magazine concerning extraordinary claims of miracles on the mission field of Indonesia. Many of these stories were investigated and reported in subsequent books on what has been called the Indonesian Revival. One such story concerns a man supposedly raised from the dead.

A missionary team was invited by a family to attend the funeral of one of the local residents. According to the report by one of the team members, when they arrived at the scene, there were more than a thousand people (Tari 1971, 66). They were sitting among the mourners when suddenly one of them claimed to have received a message from the Lord which said, "Now please go and stand around that dead person, sing songs, and I will raise him back from the dead" (Tari 1971, 66-67).

As the small band of missionaries gathered around the body of the dead person, they began to sing as they had been commanded. Nothing happened during the first few songs, but, by the sixth song the man began to move his toes. "When we sang the seventh and eighth songs, that brother woke up, looked around and smiled. . . . He just opened his mouth and said, 'Jesus has brought me back to life!'" (Tari 1971, 70).

When the man stood up and faced the crowd, he reportedly made some startling statements.

Brothers and sisters, I want to tell you something. First, life never ends when you die. I've been dead for two days and I've experienced it. Hell and heaven are real. I have experienced it. The third thing I want to tell you is, if you don't find Jesus in this life you will never go to heaven. You will be condemned to hell for sure.

Was this a miracle? Some of the circumstances are similar to the account of Jesus raising Lazarus from the dead. But even if resurrections happened in Bible times, do they still occur today?

Violent Seizure—Chemical or Diabolical?

A recurring question which arises whenever Christians are discussing the frequent occurrence of "signs and wonders" is, Could these be demonic in nature? Many Christians are reluctant to label some seemingly miraculous event as demonic or satanic. Some fear that if the event is really a miracle from God they could be guilty of blasphemy of the Spirit by calling it demonic. Certainly no one wants to mistake the movement of God for the working of demons. After all, did not Jesus rebuke His disciples for forbidding others to cast out demons (Mark 9:39)? Indeed, did He not say it was the blasphemy of the Holy Spirit to attribute the works of the Holy Spirit to the devil (Mark 3:20-30)?

A Biblical Story—Seizure or Satanic? The Gospels make frequent mention of the activity of Satan and his associates. Jesus frequently confronted individuals whom the Scriptures identify as being possessed by demons. Individuals were often afflicted in a physical manner by demonic oppression and domination.

Mark 9 records an encounter of Jesus with a boy who was reported to be possessed by a demon. His father, having heard of the healing ministry of Jesus, brought his son to be healed. The father described the condition of his son as "possessed with a spirit which makes him mute; and whenever it seizes him, it dashes him to the ground and he foams at the mouth, and grinds his teeth, and stiffens out" (Mark 9:17-18, NASB). The father told Jesus that the boy had been afflicted since childhood with frequent episodes of being thrown by the spirit into fire and then into water in an apparent effort to destroy the boy.

When Jesus commanded the boy to be brought to Him, the boy immediately went "into a convulsion, and falling to the ground, he began rolling about and foaming at the mouth" (Mark 9:20, NASB). Then Jesus rebuked the spirit and commanded it to come out of the boy. Immediately, the spirit cried out, threw the boy into "terrible convulsions," and came out of him. The lad collapsed as if dead, but Jesus took him by the hand and raised him up. He had been healed.

But was this really a miracle? Similar symptoms are not uncommon today among those who are victims of epilepsy. Indeed, in earlier times people afflicted with this disease were considered demon-possessed rather than sick. Was this the restoring of an epileptic rather than an actual account of a demon-possessed person?

Perhaps English philosopher Thomas Hobbes was correct in *Leviathan* when he said, "I see nothing at all in the Scripture that requireth a belief that demoniacs were any other thing but madmen." Can any physical disorders be attributed to demon activity? Or are all such illnesses accounted for as simply a disease for which there is a yet unknown natural explanation?

A Modern Story—Possibly Demonic? Many Christians refuse to attribute any present-day illness to the working of demons. A well-known minister relates the story of a young married couple who approached him after a meeting to find out more about Jesus. The wife had been suffering from a disorder that had been diagnosed as a very rare variety of epilepsy called myoklone.

Although the young woman had undergone frequent treatments, she seemed never to improve. "However, counseling revealed that there was one important fact that she had failed to tell the doctors. Her mother had once told her that before her birth she had tried to bring about an abortion by occult means" (Koch 1976, 9). The counselor saw a connection between the involvement of the mother in sorcery and the consequent "epileptic" episodes of the young woman. He concluded that the episodes were induced by demonic activity.

This is not an isolated incident. Another minister encountered a family in which one of the children suffered from frequent attacks of what seemed to be epileptic seizures.

After talking with other members of the family, the minister came to the conclusion that the child was really demon possessed and not suffering from epilepsy. While he was questioning the parents, the alleged occult cause of the trouble came to the surface. The child had once been cured of a certain illness by means of sorcery. And as a result of this he had developed these fits which the doctor had diagnosed as epilepsy. (Koch 1976, 8-9)

Were these experiences actual cases of demonic possession? Can demons cause physical disorders that exhibit symptoms which mimic naturally caused diseases? If this is the case, how can one distinguish between natural diseases and demonic affliction? What is more important for our consideration is this question: If demons are capable of causing physical disorders, can they also perform healings? That is, can some of the current "signs and wonders" be demonic?

Healing—Supernatural or Psychological?

The confusion over signs and wonders increases when dealing with the many afflictions that plague the human body. Some doctors claim that as many as 80 percent of their clients suffer from problems that have a psychosomatic (mind over body) component. This means that many of the physical problems for which people go to their physician are caused or aggravated by their mental or emotional state. A person who suffers from physical problems aggravated by his own mind can find sudden relief by a change in his state of mind. In these cases the cause would not be supernatural but psychosomatic. That is, the person whose mental state had sustained an illness would, when in a better frame of mind, recover.

There are a great many stories in the Bible in which individuals exercised the power to heal the sick. One example is in the Book of Acts, chapter 3. Peter and John were going to the temple at the hour of prayer when they were stopped by a man asking alms of them. This man "had been lame from his mother's womb . . . whom they used to set down every day at the gate of the temple which is called Beautiful, in order to beg alms of those who were entering the temple" (Acts 3:2, NASB).

As Peter and John entered the temple the lame man began to beg alms of them. Peter, along with John, fixed his gaze upon the man and said to him, "Look at us!" This command captured the lame man's attention, for he was expecting to receive alms from Peter and John. Peter's next words were, "I do not possess silver and gold, but what I do have I give to you: In the name of Jesus Christ the Nazarene—walk!" (v. 6, NASB). Then Peter grabbed the man by the hand and raised him up, and "immediately his feet and his ankles were strengthened. And with a leap, he stood upright and began to walk; and he entered the temple with them, walking and leaping and praising God" (Acts 3:7-8, NASB).

Of course this is by no means the only passage in the Bible

that speaks of an immediate healing. The Gospels abound with stories of Jesus healing people instantly. Nevertheless, many individuals throughout history have cast a skeptical eye at the biblical accounts. They either claim that the record is mythological or explain these events as examples of psychosomatic cures.

Dr. William A. Nolen, Chief of Surgery at Meeker County Hospital, Litchfield, Minnesota, has spent many years investigating claims of supernatural healing and has even traveled to the Philippines to investigate such claims. He claims that

when evangelical healers dramatically call on God to transmit His power through them to cure their patients' diseases, they are using the power of suggestion in the hope that it will so affect the patient's malfunctioning autonomic nervous system (the system that regulates such functions as digestion, heart rate, blood pressure, etc.) that the disease or symptoms caused by the derangement of that system will be cured. (Abell 1981, 193-194)

Many amazing healings are accomplished, including the restoration of sight, by purely psychological means (see chapter 6).

Are all healings like this, or are there any truly supernatural healings today? What does this say about many of the "signs and wonders" being performed today in evangelistic meetings and even on national TV? Are these "diseases" psychosomatically caused and psychologically cured by these "faith healers"?

For those who believe the Bible there is a problem with classifying all healings as purely psychological. Some of these "healings" resemble the biblical events of healing. Many TV evangelists claim the authority of biblical promises with reference to their healing. If we ascribe their successes to psychosomatic methods, this seems to imply that the biblical healings are not supernatural either.

Summary

We live in a veritable signs-and-wonders-land of supernormal events. There is a great deal of confusion about this maze of the miraculous. There are too many accounts to simply ignore the issue. Are these events scientific anomalies, demonic activities, or psychosomatic cures? Are they natural or supernatural? No wonder many Christians are confused.

The pressing need is for a careful, biblical examination of these "signs and wonders" to sort out the true and the false. Needed is a way to distinguish the counterfeit from the real. The rest of this book is dedicated to help in this important task.

2. What Do We Mean by "Supernatural"?

The Christian's Search for a Workable Definition

A recent TV ad invited viewers to watch an upcoming horror movie which would involve matters of the occult and witch-craft. In this ad the movie was characterized as "exploring the supernatural." This kind of advertisement betrays a general confusion about the concept of the supernatural. Almost anything unusual is called supernatural.

The very use of the word *supernatural* conjures up a variety of different images in our minds. Many people use *supernatural* to refer to occult phenomena. Others apply the word to anything that seems unexplainable. So if an event seems unexplainable in terms of anything they have ever experienced, it must be supernatural.

Also, most people look to natural science to identify the so-called supernatural. If science cannot explain an event, they sometimes call it "supernatural." But for them the supernatural is simply that for which science has not yet found an explanation. They remain skeptical about whether miracles ever really occur (see chapter 3).

Others use the term *supernatural* to denote the mystifying, the mysterious, and the occult. This usage is common in newspapers and tabloids (the *National Enquirer*, for example). It is a popular understanding of the term.

This confusion over what is in fact supernatural has contributed to the misunderstanding about the often reported experiences of signs and wonders today. In order to clarify the situation about signs and wonders it will be necessary to define exactly what we mean by a supernatural or miraculous event. *Miracle* will be defined here in a biblical sense as a special act of God in the world, a supernatural interference into nature, a special divine intervention.

A miracle is not simply an extraordinary event but one that would not have occurred without special divine intervention.

Extent of Biblical Miracles

The Bible claims to be God's revelation of His involvement in the history of the world. Because God is the Creator of all nature, He is beyond the natural, above it; He is supernatural. Nature is the way God works regularly; a miracle is the way He works on special occasions. A miracle is a divine interference into the regular course of events. Hence, it is not a natural occurrence but is truly a supernatural event.

A miracle has God's "fingerprints" on it. Whenever someone handles an object, opens a door, or touches a surface, he leaves behind fingerprints. No two persons have the same fingerprints. Therefore, experts who are able to retrieve fingerprints can match them to a particular person. When God acts in history, He leaves behind His "fingerprints." By examining the biblical record we can discover those distinctive characteristics of God's imprint.

Any event in which God is specially involved would have His fingerprints on it. For example, the Bible records that when Moses confronted the Pharaoh in Egypt he was resisted by the king's magicians. These masters of the secret arts counterfeited the first supernatural acts performed by God through Moses. But when God brought the plague of gnats upon the land, Pharaoh's sorcerers were unable to duplicate the feat (or to get rid of the gnats). They were forced to admit to Pharaoh, "This is the finger of God" (Exodus 8:19).

By examining the biblical record we can discover the characteristics of God's fingerprints. Using these distinguishing characteristics of God's special action, we will be able to discover whether a particular contemporary event measures up to this biblical definition of a supernatural act of God. In this way we can answer the question as to whether current "signs and wonders" are miracles in the biblical sense of the word.

Raising of the Dead. The most compelling act of God recorded in the Bible is the resurrection of Jesus Christ from the dead. Indeed, the resurrection of Jesus Christ is the foundation upon which believers are related to God (Romans 10:9-10). Because of His resurrection from the dead, Christians are promised salvation. The apostle Paul said Christ "was delivered up because of our sins and was raised because of our justification" (Romans 4:25, NASB). When the early disciples went into all the world to preach the gospel, the focus of their message was that Jesus had risen from the grave (see Acts 2:22-36; 3:15; 4:10; 10:39-41).

However, this is not the only instance recorded in the Bible of a person being raised from the dead by the power of God. Probably the second most noted example of the raising of the dead is the raising of Lazarus, already discussed in chapter 1. Lazarus had been dead four days when Jesus commanded that they take the stone away from the entrance to Lazarus's tomb. When the stone had been moved, Jesus called out with a loud voice, "Lazarus, come forth." Immediately Lazarus came out of the tomb, "bound hand and foot with wrappings; and his face was wrapped around with a cloth" (John 11:43-44, NASB).

The Bible relates several other such instances. In 1 Kings 17:22 Elijah raises the son of a widow at Zarephath. The passage does not say how long the child had been dead. But when Elijah cried to the Lord that the child's life be restored to him, "the life of the child returned to him and he revived" (NASB). Elisha, the successor to Elijah, also raised a young boy from the dead (2 Kings 4:33-34). In the New Testament there are at least five more instances of the dead being raised. Matthew 27:52 tells about the opening of the graves of many holy people who had died and were raised to life following the death of Jesus on the cross.

How can God's "fingerprint" be identified in these events? The most immediately obvious characteristic of a biblical miracle is that God has power over life and death. Indeed, the Bible declares that only God can give life (Deuteronomy 32:39; Job 1:21). From the raising of an individual who had just died, to the raising of holy people who had been dead for long periods of time, the Bible claims that God has power over death and the grave. The demonstration of such supernatural power is one aspect of the fingerprint of God.

Power over Nonhuman Nature. Another identifying mark of the supernatural is power over nonhuman nature. One of the most memorable incidents in the Gospels is when Jesus stilled the storm. The Sea of Galilee is positioned in the Jordan rift below sea level, with mountains to the east and west. This creates a natural condition for storms. "The cool air masses from the mountain heights rush down the steep slopes with great force causing violent eruptions of the lake. Such tempests·are not infrequent and are extremely dangerous to small craft" (Alexander 1975, 646).

The storm recorded in Matthew 8 must have been particularly· violent to have provoked such fear in these veteran fishermen. Yet Jesus was in control. While the disciples were in fear of their lives, Jesus exercised His authority over nature, rebuking the sea and winds so that it became "completely calm" (Matthew 8:26).

Of course, this is far from the only incident in which the God of the Bible demonstrates His power over nonhuman nature. Through Moses, water was turned to blood. Through Jesus, water was turned to wine. As the prophet of God, Moses parted the Red Sea so that all Israel could cross in safety. As God in human flesh, Jesus walked on top of the Sea of Galilee during a storm to show His disciples that He could not only still the sea, but that He could use it as His pathway.

The Bible is replete with examples of God's power over nonhuman nature. From the creation of matter out of nothing to the multiplying of bread to feed a multitude, the God of Scripture clearly demonstrates His absolute power over nature. God is able to transcend the natural laws which He has established, such as when He caused the sun to stop "in the middle of the sky" and delayed it from going down "about a full day" (Joshua 10:11-14).

God is also able to speed up natural processes, as when Jesus cursed the fig tree so that the disciples were amazed and said, "How did the fig tree wither at once?" (Matthew 21:20, NASB). He is also able to retard natural processes, as when He prevented the sandals on the feet of the people of Israel from wearing out, though they trod through the desert for forty years (Deuteronomy 29:5). All of these manifest God's absolute power and authority over nonhuman nature and provided us with another characteristic to identify His supernatural "fingerprint."

Power over All Kinds of Diseases. Power healing is a popular topic today, not only in Christian circles but also among the general public. Many popular magazines and papers regularly print stories about "miraculous" healings. Most of these cures are limited to nonorganic, psychosomatic types of sicknesses. Yet the Bible records God's power over all kinds of diseases. So in order to measure up to a biblical miracle, current signs and wonders will have to include all kinds of diseases.

The Gospels are filled with accounts of Jesus' power over all kinds of diseases. Indeed, it is frequently stated in the Gospels that Jesus went through the countryside teaching, preaching, and healing every disease and sickness (Matthew 4:23; 9:35; 10:1). Jesus healed those who were crippled. In John 5:1-9 Jesus healed a man who had been an invalid for thirty-eight years so that he was able at once to pick up his bed and walk. Jesus was able to heal a man who had been born blind (John 9:1-7). He stopped the issue of blood that had plagued a woman for twelve years (Mark 5:25-34). He healed crippled hands. He restored hearing. He caused the dumb to speak. Clearly Jesus demonstrated His authority and power over all kinds of human diseases and sicknesses.

Many prophets and apostles were used by God to heal the sick. Healing was an aspect of the ministry of many Old Testament prophets. For example, in 2 Kings 20 we find the account of Hezekiah praying for healing. God told Isaiah to tell Hezekiah that He had heard Hezekiah's prayer and that he would be healed.

Peter was the instrument on several occasions to heal those

who were sick. Paul was also an instrument in the hands of God for the healing of many (see Acts 3). Acts 14 describes an instance of Paul's healing ministry: "At Lystra there was sitting a certain man, without strength in his feet, lame from his mother's womb, who had never walked. This man was listening to Paul as he spoke, who, when he had fixed his gaze upon him, and had seen that he had faith to be made well, said with a loud voice, 'Stand upright on your feet,' and he leaped up and began to walk" (Acts 14:8-10, NASB).

In the Bible, God clearly demonstrated His absolute power over all kinds of diseases. Not even death can defy His authority. Through His instruments in both the Old and the New Testaments God repeatedly exercised His power over human sicknesses and afflictions and provided us with still another characteristic by which we can identify His fingerprint.

Nature of Biblical Miracles

The brief look at some of the supernatural acts of God in the Scriptures provides us with some of the basic characteristics which will enable us to recognize God's fingerprint. Let us now identify some of these characteristics more specifically.

Miracles Are Always Successful. One of the most obvious characteristics of God's supernatural acts is that they are always successful. When Jesus undertook the task of healing an individual, no illness was too severe, no sickness had done too much damage, no affliction had its grip on a victim too tightly. Jesus was always successful. Indeed, many hopeful victims cried to Jesus, "Lord, if you are willing, you can make me clean." Those who were afflicted with all kinds of diseases realized that Jesus was able to heal them if He wanted to. Never in His ministry did He ever fail to successfully heal anyone He tried to heal.

Indeed, the Bible records that God is always successful in His efforts. Diseases always vanish at His command, demons always flee at His order, nature is always open to His intervention. The fact that God is always able to successfully accomplish His will is the foundation of our assurance. Even the pagan King Nebuchadnezzar finally realized this about the Most High: "No one can ward off His hand or say to Him, 'What hast Thou done?'" (Daniel 4:35, NASB).

This is an important characteristic of the fingerprint of God which bears repeating. *The supernatural acts of God in the Bible were and are always successful.* That is, God always accomplished what He intended to accomplish. If He desired to heal someone, they were completely healed. There are no exceptions (see Appendix 2). Jesus never failed.

Miracles Are Immediate. Not only were God's miraculous acts always successful, but, with specific regard to the healing ministry of Jesus, the results were always immediate. There were no instances of gradual improvement over a few days. Jesus commanded the invalid to "Arise, take up your pallet and walk," and "immediately the man became well" (John 5:8, NASB).

When Jesus healed Peter's mother-in-law (Matthew 8:14-15, NASB), "she arose, and began to wait on Him." A fever makes a person very weak, and even when the fever is gone, there is a length of time in which the patient gradually regains his strength. Not so when Jesus healed Peter's mother-in-law. One moment she was in bed, weak from a fever. The next moment she was completely recovered, so that her strength had returned and she was able to serve Him.

In Peter's ministry in Acts 3 we see God healing a lame man instantly at Peter's hand. "Peter said, 'I do not possess silver and gold, but what I do have I give to you: In the name of Jesus Christ the Nazarene—walk!' And seizing him by the right hand, he raised him up; and immediately his feet and ankles were strengthened" (Acts 3:6-7, NASB). There was no lapse of time over which the man gradually improved. The restoration of this man's health was instantaneous and complete.

Miracles Have No Relapses. One very notable and often overlooked characteristic of biblical accounts of healing is that there are no known relapses. In all of Jesus' healings there is not a single account of a relapse. Of course, eventually they all died as do all other humans (Romans 5:12). Only the final resurrection will "cure" this malady (John 5:5).

Significant in these healings is the absence of any accusations from Jesus' enemies. The Pharisees frequently attempted to discredit Jesus in the eyes of the people. Had they known of the relapse of one of those whom Jesus had healed they most certainly would have exploited it to further their goal of destroying Him.

In Luke 5:17-32 Jesus made an explicit connection between His power to heal and His authority to forgive sins. Jesus said, "But in order that you may know that the Son of Man has authority on earth to forgive sins . . ." at which time He turned to the paralyzed man and commanded, "I say to you, rise, and take up your stretcher and go home. And at once he rose up before them, and took up what he had been lying on, and went home, glorifying God" (Luke 5:25, NASB). This miracle was presented as an outward evidence for Jesus' claim to have authority to forgive sins. Consequently, the relapse of anyone whom Jesus had healed would have been a devastating weapon in the hands of His enemies.

Neither the Bible nor extrabiblical history record a relapse of anyone whom Jesus healed. This is yet another characteristic of the fingerprint of God. Not only were God's biblical miracles always successful and immediate, but when God healed someone, it was permanent.

Miracles Give Confirmation of God's Messenger. God did not arbitrarily perform miracles. Rather, there was always a purpose for His supernatural acts. One of the most important purposes for the working of miracles was as a confirmation of some individual as a messenger of God. Thus His sermon was confirmed by a sign; the message was attested by the miracle.

The use of miracles to confirm God's spokesmen is graphically portrayed in the calling of Moses in Exodus 3 and 4. In these chapters God speaks to Moses and commands him, "Come now, and I will send you to Pharaoh, so that you may bring my people, the sons of Israel, out of Egypt" (Exodus 3:10, NASB). But Moses objected saying, "Who am I, that I should go to Pharaoh, and that I should bring the sons of Israel out of Egypt?" God promised to be with Moses and told him to tell the elders of Israel, "The Lord, the God of your fathers . . . has appeared to me" (Exodus 3:16, NASB). Moses objected again, saying, "What if they will not believe me, or listen to what I say? For they may say, 'The LORD has not appeared to you'" (Exodus 4:1, NASB).

In response to Moses' question, God instructed him to perform certain "signs" (Exodus 4:17) in the presence of Israel "that they may believe that the Lord, the God of their fathers . . . has appeared to you" (Exodus 4:5, NASB). Clearly, performing miraculous signs by Moses authenticated him as the one God had sent to deliver Israel from bondage.

This was also true with reference to Jesus. When He was confronted by the questioning multitude He responded, "Why then do you accuse me of blasphemy because I said, 'I am God's Son?' Do not believe me unless I do what my Father does. But if I do it, even though you do not believe me, believe the miracles, that you may know and understand that the Father is in me, and I in the Father" (John 10:36-38). Jesus pointed to His miracles as evidence that His claims were true.

In Acts 2:22 we find this same reasoning. Peter told the multitude that Jesus "was a man accredited by God to you by miracles, wonders and signs, which God did among you through him, as you yourselves know." And one of the most succinct statements about miracles confirming Jesus' claim to have been sent from God was made by Nicodemus in John. "Rabbi, we know you are a teacher who has come from God. For no one could perform the miraculous signs you are doing if God were not with him" (John 3:2).

Miraculous signs and wonders were performed by individuals in the Bible as a testimony and as evidence that they had been sent by God. The miraculous works confirmed the claims they each made to be messengers of God. Hebrews 2:3-4 states unequivocally that "this salvation, which was first announced by the Lord, was confirmed to us by those who heard him. God also testified to it by signs, wonders and various miracles, and gifts of the Holy Spirit distributed according to his will." Just as the old covenant was "binding" when confirmed by miracles through Moses, even so the message of Christ and the apostles was officially confirmed through their miracles. God's servants are confirmed by God's signs. His messengers are confirmed by His miracles.

The supernatural acts of God in human history have left His fingerprints. The biblical record has preserved this information, and from it we are able to identify those characteristics that will enable us to recognize God at work in a supernatural way in our world. Any alleged "supernatural" events that fall short of these distinguishing traits are not truly miraculous in the biblical sense, however much they may otherwise manifest God's providential hand.

Summary

This brief examination of biblical miracles has yielded some of the basic characteristics of what the Bible presents as the supernatural acts of God. Let us state these once again. First, miracles are always successful. The extent of biblical miracles includes power over death, power over nonhuman nature, and power over all kinds of diseases. Next, the nature of biblical miracles involves the facts that they were always immediate, never gradual. Further, there were no relapses, and they were used to confirm a messenger of God.

There are no exceptions to this pattern (see Appendix 2). These characteristics provide a framework upon which we can build biblical understanding of the supernatural. They are the particular characteristics of the "fingerprint" of God. Although miracles possess some additional characteristics, any supposed miraculous event that violates these characteristics is not a miraculous event in the biblical sense.

3. Skeptical or Open-minded?
The Bias of Science

In the Bible, a miracle is a supernatural intervention into the world. It is a special act of God that is immediate and unique. Biblical miracles witness to God's control over the natural world. Healings were always immediate, always successful, included all kinds of diseases, and had no relapses. This is how miracles are described in the Bible. But did these miraculous events really happen? The modern "enlightened" scientific response is negative. Why? The following quotations answer that question.

Science is about unbroken, natural regularity. It does not admit miracles.—Michael Ruse in *Science Technology and Human Values*, Summer 1982.

The central axiom of our epic is that the Universe must have been formed by natural laws which are still discoverable today.—James S. Trefil, "Closing in on Creation," *Smithsonian*, May 1983

Science is "atheistic" because it is guided by natural law, must explain its conclusions by reference to natural law, . . . Thus it cannot possibly have anything to do with God.—Langdon Gilkey, "The Theologian's Case against Creationism," *The Reader*, 19 March 1982

Such a concept [creationism] is not science because it depends upon a supernatural intervention which is not guided by natural law.—Statement in U.S. Federal Court, McClain v. Arkansas, 5 January 1982

Since the supernatural must remain forever outside the context of man's knowledge, a "supernatural explanation" is a contradiction in terms.—George H. Smith, Atheism: The Case against God

So goes the modern scientific attitude toward miracles. Miracles, these scholars believe, are simply contrary to science.

Science and the Supernatural

Before the rise of modern science it was common to believe in miracles. During the Dark Ages, volcanoes, earthquakes, and meteors were often explained as having a miraculous origin. But science has since discovered natural explanations for all of these events. Christians once believed that the earth's crust was the result of a supernatural judgment of God at the Flood. Now geologists have identified the natural processes of sedimentation. Christians also believed that God supernaturally created every living species. But most scientists since Darwin believe that evolution can explain how species evolve by natural processes.

Sir Isaac Newton, discoverer of the law of gravity, invoked God to explain the unusual orbit of planets. But later the French astronomer, Pierre Laplace, was able to explain this by purely natural laws. When Napoleon asked Laplace why God was not mentioned in his book, he replied "Sire, we have no need of that hypothesis." Modern science is naturalistic. It does not admit the supernatural into its domain. The unexplained is not unexplainable. Scientists hold that the apparent gaps in nature are really only gaps in our understanding of nature.

Benedict Spinoza (1632–1677). One of the first modern thinkers to attack the supernatural was the Jewish naturalist,

Benedict Spinoza. Arguing from Newton's concept of a universal law of nature, Spinoza insisted in his *Tractatus Theologica-politicus* that "nothing, then, comes to pass in nature in contravention to her universal laws; nay, nothing does not agree with them and follow from them, for . . . she keeps a fixed and immutable order." In fact, for Spinoza "a miracle, whether in contravention to, or beyond, nature, is a mere absurdity." Spinoza was dogmatic about the impossibility of miracles. He proclaimed, "We may, then, be absolutely certain that every event which is truly described in Scripture necessarily happened, like everything else, according to natural laws" (Spinoza 1883, 1.83, 87, 92). That is, nature "keeps a fixed and immutable order." For everything "necessarily happened . . . according to natural laws." And "nothing comes to pass in nature in contravention to her universal laws. . . ." To believe otherwise "is a mere absurdity" (Spinoza 1883, 83).

Spinoza's argument can be summarized as follows:
1. Miracles are violations of natural laws.
2. Natural laws are immutable.
3. It is impossible for immutable laws to be violated.
4. Therefore, miracles are impossible.

It is clear that the second statement is the crucial one: natural laws are immutable. Just how does one know this? From a strictly common-sense point of view, the answer might be, We know this by universal observation. That is, we always observe physical objects fall in accordance with Newton's law of gravitation. There are no known exceptions. But a miracle would be an exception. Hence, miracles are contrary to universal scientific observation.

Few scientists today would agree with Spinoza's outdated belief that natural law is immutable. Modern physicists think of natural laws as being only highly probable descriptions, not absolutely unbreakable laws. Nonetheless, Spinoza's antisupernatural legacy continues.

David Hume (1711–1776). Perhaps the most enduring argument against miracles came a century after Spinoza from the Scottish skeptic, David Hume. He boasted of this argument: "I flatter myself that I have discovered an argument . . .

which, if just, will, with the wise and learned, be an everlasting check to all kinds of superstitious delusion, and consequently will be useful as long as the world endures" (Hume 1902, 10.1.118).

Just what is this "final" argument against the miraculous? In Hume's own words:

1. "A miracle is a violation of the laws of nature."
2. "Firm and unalterable experience has established these laws."
3. "A wise man proportions his belief to the evidence."
4. Therefore, "the proof against miracles . . . is as entire as any argument from experience can possibly be imagined" (Hume, 118-123).

In this argument the key statement is the second one which Hume explains as follows: "There must, therefore, be a uniform experience against every miraculous event. Otherwise the event would not merit that appellation." So "nothing is esteemed a miracle if it ever happened in the common course of nature" (Hume, 101.122-123).

Here again the essence of the argument depends on repeated observations. For the common course of nature provides us with uniform experience of natural regularities. So Hume's argument rests upon the regularity of nature as opposed to the claim for highly irregular events (such as miracles). And since science deals only with the regular, not the singular, it cannot admit miracles.

Antony Flew (b. 1923). One of the most famous contemporary attacks on miracles comes from British philosopher Antony Flew. Flew notes that "Hume was primarily concerned, not with the question of fact, but with that of evidence. The problem was how the occurrence of a miracle could be proved, rather than whether any such events had ever occurred." However, adds Flew, "Our sole ground for characterizing the reported occurrence as miraculous is at the same time a sufficient reason for calling it physically impossible." Why is this so? Because "the critical historian, confronted with some story of a miracle, will usually dismiss it out of hand" (Flew 1967, 5.346-353). On what grounds?

Flew's answer can be summarized this way:
1. Miracles are by nature particular and unrepeatable.
2. Natural events are by nature general and repeatable.
3. Now, in practice, the evidence for the general and repeatable is always greater than that for the particular and unrepeatable.
4. Therefore, in practice, the evidence will always be greater against miracles than for them.

Like the arguments of Spinoza and Hume, the key to Flew's objection to miracles is the statement (no. 3) that counts as greater evidence events which are regular or repeatable. For science by its very nature is not based on the exceptional or the odd but on the normal and the usual. And since miracles are exceptional events, they cannot be allowed in the domain of science.

The common thread in all these arguments against miracles is the belief that science is based on regularities, not singularities. That is, a scientific understanding is only possible if something happens over and over so that a pattern develops. If something happens only once, there is no pattern. Regularity, then, is the basis of a scientific understanding. Therefore, science as such can never accept the miraculous. Thus the principle of regularity seems to be the common element in the antisupernatural arguments.

The Nature of Science

Science and Repetition. Science is firmly based on regular, repeatable events. Even when an unusual event occurs scientists do not consider it part of a scientific explanation. Thus experiments that cannot be repeated are given little or no validity. At least, unrepeatable events are never made the basis for an operational law of science. One thinker argued the following:
1. No event can be attributed to a rational agent unless its occurrence is regular and repeatable.
2. Miracles are by nature not regular or repeatable.
3. Therefore, no miracle can be attributed to any rational agent (e.g., to God) (Chryssides 1975, 319-327).

The crux of this objection to miracles is what he called the "repeatability requirement" (Chryssides, 322). Unless an event can be repeated over and over again we have no right to claim we know who (or what) caused it. For example, a person should not make a causal connection between a golfer's new club and a once-in-a-life-time hole-in-one he shot with it. Rather, we would consider it a lucky shot. Scientific analysis is not based on fluke relations but on repeated connections. For unless there is a direct correlation between the presence and absence of the cause and the presence and absence of the effect, then scientific basis is lacking for believing it is the cause. Science is not based on one-time happenings, known as singularities.

This same point applies whether the cause is a natural force or an intelligent being. Certainly no one would believe that there is a scientifically established causal connection between one's ability to pick a winning horse and a one-time win at the racetrack. For unless an intelligent being can do it over and over, we would believe the result was a matter of luck, not a matter of scientific intelligence.

Likewise, no one would believe that the sentence "Eat them; they are delicious," spelled out in alphabet cereal on the table, resulted from a fan blowing on the cereal box. Unless the fan does this repeatedly with randomly dropped letters, we would consider this one-time event an anomaly. If it is a one-time event, then no scientific causal connection will be drawn between the apparent message and the fan. It would simply be considered a fluke.

So whether we are dealing with nonintelligent or intelligent causes, there must be a repeatedly observed relationship before the connection can be considered scientifically based. But this repeated relation is precisely what we do not—indeed, cannot—have with miracles because they are one-time events. Hence, by nature, singularities (such as miracles) would seem to be ruled out of the realm of science.

Science and Regularity. Science is grounded on the principle of regularity, which by its very nature seems to be against miracles. To understand this approach let us first try to pinpoint the basic problem in the arguments against miracles.

The essence of the argument goes like this:

1. Only what is observed to occur over and over again can be the basis for a scientific understanding of what caused the event.
2. Singular events like miracles are not repeated over and over again.
3. Therefore, there is no scientific basis for a singularity such as a miracle.

It is because of this that scientists are so militantly opposed to teaching there was a supernatural creation of the world. This was demonstrated when seventy-two Nobel Prize-winning scientists appealed to the Supreme Court not to allow the teaching of creation in public schools. The court later agreed with them (Edwards, June 19, 1987).

Does Science Exclude Miracles?

However, this deeply rooted bias in the scientific community is misplaced. The first and most obvious problem with their argument against miracles is that it proves too much. For if the argument is valid, then it would prove that there is no scientific basis for some events that are considered to be scientific by these same scientists. For modern science has its own set of one-time events (singularities). It believes in a one-time origin of the universe, in a one-time origin of life. Further, most scientists are evolutionists who believe in a one-time achievement of the great evolutionary transitions (from lower to higher forms). But all of these fall into the same overall class that miracles do: they are all unrepeated singularities.[1]

So if scientists are going to exclude miracles because they are singular events, then they will also have to exclude some of their own widely held beliefs about origins, including evolution itself.

The origin of the universe was a one-time event. The Big Bang theory is considered by most astronomers to be the

1. Of course, not all singularities are miracles. But all miracles fall into the class of singularities. And miracles cannot be eliminated because they are singularities any more than can other singularities that are believed to be purely natural.

most viable scientific explanation of the origin of the universe. According to this view, the whole material universe exploded into being at a specific moment in the distant past. But so far as the scientific evidence goes, the Big Bang occurred only once. It has not been repeated. It is a singularity. Hence, if the scientist insists that only regular and repeated events can be scientific, then one of the most widely held scientific views on the origin of the universe is also unscientific.

The origin of life is a one-time event. Many scientists believe in the spontaneous generation of first life from nonliving chemicals. But the spontaneous generation of life has not happened over and over again. What is more, we do not observe it happening spontaneously over and over again in the present. But if repeatability in the present is essential to a scientific understanding of an event, then the belief in spontaneous generation is not scientific either (see Jastrow 1977, 63). So on the same grounds they would eliminate miracles, they set up a kind of miraculous one-time event of their own. After all, to believe something came from nothing and that the living came from the nonliving are really miracles. Call it what you may, a rose by any other name is still a rose. And a miracle by any other name is still miraculous. The origin of first life is a singular event accepted by naturalistic scientists. So they cannot exclude miracles because they are singularities and yet at the same time accept singularities, such as the spontaneous one-time beginning of the first living thing.

Origins of new life forms are one-time events. The same logic applies to the naturalistic theory of large-scale evolution. According to this belief, the evolutionary movement between the great categories of living things occurred only once. For example, fish evolved into reptiles only once. Reptiles evolved into birds only once, and so on. These events have never happened again. Yet naturalistic scientists believe it is scientific to speak of the origin of these new life forms. Many even call evolution a "fact," not merely a theory (Asimov 1981, 86).

But if it is unscientific to believe in singularities, then it would also be unscientific to believe in large scale evolution, for it involves unrepeated singularities. In short, the naturalist's argument against singularities proves too much; it proves that even some of his naturalistic explanations, such as evolution, are not science either. Or, put another way, it is inconsistent for the antisupernaturalists to argue against miracles because they are one-time events, only to replace them with unique one-time events of their own.

Is the Object of Science Always a Regularity? Everyone readily admits that science is *based on* regularity, or repeated events. But as was just seen, this does not mean it cannot have a singular event as its *object*. For example, it is the regular laws, such as the Second Law of Thermodynamics, that lead scientists to believe the universe is running down and must have had a beginning. But this beginning to which it points is a singular event. Thus while the *basis* of this scientific reasoning is regularity, its *object* is a singularity.

Likewise, it is scientific observation of the regular that leads us to believe that the kind of complex information found in a book always comes from an intelligent being. This, however, does not hinder scientists from believing that a singular message of complex information from outer space on a radio telescope would lead to the conclusion that there were intelligent beings out there. Carl Sagan, for example, believed that "the receipt of a single message from space" would show that there are intelligent beings out there (Sagan 1979, 275).

Here again the object of the scientific search is a singular event. But the basis for concluding that only intelligent beings produce that kind of complex information is a regularity. For a regularly observed connection between intelligent causes and that kind of complex information is the grounds upon which we attribute an intelligent cause to that single message.

Scientists do not hesitate to posit an intelligent cause when they discover a singular artifact. For example, discovering only one arrowhead leads scientists to conclude an intelligent being formed it. Likewise, a single piece of pottery or art leads archaeologists to posit an intelligent cause for it.

On an everyday level we often reason that there was an intelligent cause for something we see only once. "Drink Pepsi" written in the sky or "John loves Mary" written in the sand always invoke an intelligent cause. These conclusions are based on the same principle used by scientists, the principle of regularity. Whenever we see a certain kind of cause produce a certain kind of effect, then when we come upon a singular instance of this later, we also assume it had an intelligent cause.

For instance, we only need to see one Mount Rushmore (object) to know it had an intelligent cause because we have seen many sculptors do similar things before (basis). The same is true of other unique things, such as the Great Pyramids and China's Great Wall. Purely natural laws are never observed regularly producing these kinds of things. But we see intelligent beings doing similar things all the time. So on the basis of the regular observations that it takes an intelligent cause to produce the kind of complex information in a living cell, it is scientific to assume that the singular event of the beginning of life was also caused by an intelligent cause.

In summary, the argument against miracles confuses the *basis* of science which is always some regular connection and the *object* of science that can be some singular event, such as the origin of the universe, the origin of first life, or even a message from outer space (see Geisler 1987, chapter 5).

Science Points to the Supernatural

Contrary to popular opinion, science does not destroy miracles; rather, it points to them. Scientific evidence does not eliminate them; it naturally evokes them. For the very principle of regularity on which science is based calls for an intelligent cause beyond purely natural processes for the first living thing and the entire cosmos.

So far as the scientific evidence goes, the universe came into being out of nothing. For the universe is running down and, hence, must have had a beginning. But things do not pop into existence out of nothing without a cause. This beginning of the universe points to a cause beyond the natural world. But the only kind of cause that exists beyond the natural world is a supernatural cause (i.e., God). So rather than disproving the supernatural, the scientific evidence points to the supernatural. Even the agnostic astronomer, Robert Jastrow, confessed, "There are what I or anyone would call supernatural forces at work is now, I think, a scientifically proven fact" (Jastrow 1982, 18).

But is the supernatural cause of the universe an intelligent cause or just an impersonal force? The answer to this comes from examining other evidence. One such line of evidence involves the "anthropic principle." According to the anthropic principle (from *anthropos*, man), the universe was from the very instant of its creation amazingly suited for the eventual emergence of human life on earth. In short, the stage was preset for man from the very moment of the Big Bang. If the arrangement of atoms had been off in even the most minute way, human life would never have arrived. Commenting on this principle, Robert Jastrow said,

The anthropic principle is the most interesting development next to the proof of the creation, and it is even more interesting because it seems to say that science itself has proven, as a hard fact, that this universe was made, was designed, for man to live in. It's a very theistic result. (Jastrow 1982, 17)

It is a very "theistic" (from *theos*, God) result because it is best explained by intelligent advanced planning. That is, the universe was preplanned by some super intelligence for the existence of human beings. As the famous American astronomer, Allan Sandage, put it:

The world is too complicated in all its parts and interconnections to be due to chance alone. I am convinced that the existence of life with all its order in each of its organisms is simply too well put together. Each part of a living thing depends on all its other parts to function. How does each part know? How is each part specified at conception? The more one learns of biochemistry the more unbelievable it becomes unless there is some type of organizing principle. (Sandage 1985, 54)

This leads us to a second singularity that points to an intelligent cause. Scientists now know that even a one-cell organism is a very complex creature. In fact, the genetic information in the simplest single cell animal would equal that in a whole volume of the *Encyclopedia Britannica*. And there is striking new evidence that the kind of complex information in the genetic code of living things (called "specified complexity") is exactly the same as that found in human language, which is known to come from intelligent beings.

Recently a scientist applied the knowledge developed from the study of human languages (called Information Theory) to the four-letter alphabet of the genetic code in living things. He found that it was "mathematically identical" to that of a written language (Yockey 1981, 16). But it is known that the complex information in a written language results from an intelligent being. Even simple messages like "Drink Coke" or "I love you, Mary" are known to come from intelligent beings. Many scientists, like Sagan, would accept a "single" message from outer space as proof of an intelligent civilization. But the first living cell must have had this same kind of complex information in it. Therefore, it is only reasonable to conclude that there was an intelligent supernatural cause of the first living thing.

Looking at the evidence of the specified complexity in a single cell organism, one former atheist, Sir Fred Hoyle, concluded that believing there was no intelligent cause of the first living thing is like believing that a Boeing 747 resulted from a tornado raging through a junk yard! (See Hoyle 1981, especially pp. 3, 6, 24-26, 48.) A one-cell animal is as complex as a dictionary. And no scientist would believe a person who told him that their *Webster's Dictionary* was produced by an explosion in a printing shop!

The consistent evidence that only an intelligent cause produces this kind of intelligent information should lead intelligent people to posit an Intelligent Cause of the first living thing. Here again the scientific evidence points to the Supernatural (i.e., to God).

Summary

Many modern scientists object to miracles because they believe they are one-time events (singularities) and that science deals only with regularities. Yet these same scientists accept many singularities themselves. Most of them believe the universe came into existence with a Big Bang, an event that has not repeated since. Most of them believe life emerged from nonlife once by spontaneous generation and has not recurred again. All of these same scientists believe in some form of evolution by which there was an unrepeated development of higher forms from lower ones. But all these unrepeated events are accepted, while at the same time miracles are rejected because they are singularities. This is obviously inconsistent.

Likewise, many scientists argue that the supernatural has no place in science; science deals only with the natural. Yet the scientific evidence points to a supernatural beginning of the natural world. Indeed, it points to an intelligent cause of life with all of its complexity. So following the very principles of science we are led back to an intelligent, supernatural cause of the universe and life. With this we have come full circle to where science began—with God. At the very dawn of modern science Sir Isaac Newton wrote:

It is not to be conceived that mere mechanical causes could give birth to so many regular motions. . . .This most beautiful system of the sun, planets, and comets, could only proceed from the counsel and dominion of an intelligent and powerful Being. (Newton 1952, 369)

These words are as true today as when Newton wrote them. True, science does not negate the supernatural; it needs it. But if there is a supernatural cause, then supernatural events are possible. Indeed, if God exists then the big miracles have already happened, because bringing the universe into existence out of nothing is the greatest miracle of all. For example, making much bread out of little bread (which Jesus did in feeding the five-thousand) is no problem for Someone who can make something out of nothing. Other miracles in the Bible are small by comparison to the miracle of creation to which the scientific evidence strongly points. If the first verse of the Bible is so strongly confirmed, then all other miracles recorded in it are credible. And the amazing thing is that even non-Christian scientists, like Jastrow, have been forced to conclude that

the astronomical evidence leads to a biblical view of the origin of the world. The details differ, but the essential elements in the astronomical and biblical accounts of Genesis are the same: the chain of events leading to man commenced suddenly and sharply at a definite moment in time, in a flash of light and energy. (Jastrow 1978, 14)

But if there was a beginning, then there was a Beginner. If there was a creation, then there was a Creator. And if God exists, then other miracles are possible. As C. S. Lewis concluded, "If we admit God, must we admit Miracle? Indeed, indeed, you have no security against it. That is the bargain" (Lewis 1947, 109).

4. Truly Supernatural or Merely Unusual?

A woman was dancing on a crowded floor in Chelmsford, England, when suddenly she burst into flames. Within a few moments there was nothing left of her but ashes. Coroner Leslie Beccles announced, "In all my experience I've never come across any case as mysterious as this" (North 1976, 7).

On December 5, 1945, Flight 19 took off from Fort Lauderdale Naval Air Station on a routine patrol. Less than two hours later the commander reported that he was lost over the Florida Keys. A search plane was dispatched to help. Neither plane ever returned. Both were swallowed up in the mysterious Bermuda Triangle (Kole 1984, 87-88).

Explain That to Me!

"All that glitters is not gold," said Shakespeare. Every mystery is not a miracle. Not everything supernormal is supernatural. There are many things that are odd; but all are not of God. The world is filled with unusual and incredible occurrences. The vast majority of them have nothing to do with the miraculous. They have purely natural explanations.

The unexplained is not necessarily the unexplainable. There are many natural phenomena I can't explain, but trained scientists can. The odd does not necessarily call for God. Just because we do not understand something does not mean that there is no explanation for it.

Many people down through the centuries have fallen victim to the "God-of-the-gaps" error. They have assumed (wrongly) that because we cannot explain some unusual events that they must have a supernatural cause. Unfortunately, the gaps often turned out to be gaps in human understanding, not events demanding divine intervention. Examples of "God-of-the-gaps" thinking are numerous.

Sir Isaac Newton posited God's intervention to explain the irregular motion of some planets. Later, the French scientist Pierre Laplace explained the motions by purely natural means.

Some scientists once claimed that the earth's crust was a result of supernatural divine judgment. But later pioneer geologists James Hutton and Charles Lyell developed purely natural explanations of the earth's history.

Many people once believed that meteors, eclipses, and earthquakes were supernatural occurrences. Now all scientists and informed persons know they occur by natural causes.

Until recently the flight of the bumblebee was a mystery. With such small wings and such a large body, flight seemed to be an aerodynamic impossibility. But faith in natural explanations paid off. Eventually a scientist discovered a "power pack" on bumblebees that enables their wings to move at tremendous speeds that can overcome this aerodynamic difficulty.

There are still many unexplained mysteries in nature. For example, scientists do not know how to explain how life grows around the dark hydrothermo vents in the depths of the sea. But their belief that a natural cause will yet be found is not unreasonable for two reasons. First, many other mysteries of nature's operations have yielded to further research. Second, events that are regular or repeatable are by their nature natural events, whether or not they are presently understood. For natural science deals with the regular and repeatable (see chapter 3).

Miracles by definition fall only into the category of the singular and unrepeatable. Since the bumblebee flies regularly, there was no need to invoke God, even when we did not know how it flew. The same is true of earthquakes and eclipses, even though they do not occur at the same interval of regularity that bees fly. When enough is known about the regular pattern involved, sound predictions can be made as to when the next one will occur. To be sure, earthquakes and other phenomena of nature, such as meteors, are unusual events. They are so unusual that some primitive peoples who do not understand science still ascribe supernatural significance to these kinds of events. However, their conclusion is based on ignorance. It is a "God-of-the-gaps" mistake.

Some people operate with this same mentality today. They assume too quickly that everything unusual is supernatural. The truth is there are many kinds of unusual or odd events that have purely natural explanations. There are also unusual events that are not miracles and yet are not physical anomalies, such as magical tricks, psychosomatic cures, and psychic powers. (See chart on following page.)

From the chart it is clear that all that is unusual is not supernatural. Since the other categories of unusual events are treated in other chapters, the focus here will primarily be on natural or psychological explanations of unusual occurrences.

How to Explain the Unusual

The Bermuda Triangle. Volumes have been written on the mysterious disappearances of vessels within the "Bermuda Triangle." This section of the western Atlantic extends from Bermuda on the north to southern Florida and east through the Bahamas to Puerto Rico. Author of a best-selling book, *The Bermuda Triangle,* Charles Berlitz, declares that this area is where

more than 100 planes and ships have literally vanished into thin air, most of them since 1945, and where more than 1,000 lives have been lost in the past twenty-six years, without a single body or even a piece of wreckage from the vanishing planes or ships have been found. Disappearances continue to occur with apparently increasing frequency, in spite of the fact that the seaways and airways are today more traveled, searches are more

CATEGORIES OF THE UNUSUAL

There are at least six different categories of unusual events. They can be summarized as follows:*

NAME	DESCRIPTION	POWER	EXAMPLE	TRAITS
Anomaly	Freaks of Nature	Physical	Bumblebee	Natural event, has a pattern
Magic	Deception, fooling	Human	Rabbit in hat	Unnatural, man-controlled
Psychosomatic	Mind over matter	Mental	Psychosomatic cures	Requires faith, can fail, some sickness
Demonic	Evil powers	Supernormal	Demonic influence	Evil, falsehood, occult, limited
Providential	Prearranged events	Divine	Fog at Normandy	Naturally explained, spiritual context
Miracle	Divine act	Supernatural	Raising the dead	Never fails, immediate, lasts, brings glory to God

*In addition to these normal kinds of unusual events, there are also abnormal ones such as hallucinations, whether they result from hallucinogenic drugs or other means.

thorough, and records are more carefully kept. (Quoted in Kole 1984, 83)

There have been numerous ingenious attempts to explain these phenomena, including tidal waves, fireball lightning, time-space warp, electromagnetic waves, and attacks by UFOs! One of the more sensible explanations is found in a book by a former faculty member of Arizona State University, Larry Kusche. It is entitled, *The Bermuda Triangle Mystery—Solved.*

First, Kusche notes that 15 to 20 percent of the reported occurrences never happened. For example, the October 1978 disappearance of a forty-foot cabin cruiser (reported by Berlitz) apparently never happened. Evidence: 1) The three people aboard were never named and apparently never lived. 2) The local newspapers carried no report of the incident. 3) The local Coast Guard has no record of it. In brief, there is no evidence it ever happened.

Second, 25 to 30 percent of the reported disappearances did not occur within the boundaries of the Bermuda Triangle. Some were in the Gulf of Mexico and others in the far reaches of the Atlantic. For example, the American *Globemaster* that disappeared in March 1950 actually exploded about six hundred miles southwest of Ireland!

Third, most disappearances occurred, not on a calm clear day, but in severe weather. For example, the disappearance of the *Marine Sulphur Queen* was due to "the ship's weakened structure and the [bad] weather conditions as described in the report of the Coast Guard investigation" (Kole 1984, 85).

The most legendary instance in the Bermuda Triangle is explained in Larry Kusche's book, *The Disappearance of Flight 19.* Retracing the flight, Kusche noticed that haze caused by humid air causes the ocean and sky to blend, causing a disorienting effect. Visibility that day was known to be poor, and a slight navigational error would have placed the plane two hundred miles east of Florida and into rough seas. The loss of the search plane is also explainable. The Marines sometimes called these "flying gas tanks" because of the two thousand gallons of fuel they carried. One exploded over Greece. Fumes were occasionally present inside the plane. Even a cigarette or auxiliary generator could have ignited them. Thus the mystery of the Bermuda Triangle begins to disappear under further and more careful scrutiny. When the facts are known the mystery evaporates.

The Bridey Murphy Case. Through hypnosis a woman recalled her past life as a woman—Bridey Murphy—in seventeenth- or eighteenth-century Ireland. She spoke Gaelic, a language she had never learned, and even described details of the coastline and culture she knew in this previous life. For many this was taken as proof of the paranormal. Others were skeptical.

As it turns out their skepticism was justified. Researchers Harold Rosen (Rosen 1956) and Martin Gardner (Gardner 1974) debunked the reincarnation hypothesis. They showed that Bridey Murphy never existed at all but was a figment of a child's imagination. Research revealed that the woman was reared by her grandmother, who spoke Gaelic and who possessed books about old Ireland. These books had been read to her as a child, and her grandmother taught her Gaelic. Apparently she had forgotten about this as she grew up, but it was not totally erased from her memory. Later, under hypnosis, she recalled what she had learned as a child. Again, the mystery dissolves under the light of further research. The woman was not, so far as anyone knows, being a deliberate fraud. (We will look at fraud closely in the next chapter.) Rather, through some perfectly natural mental processes she came to remember things that had been deeply hidden in her mind. So in this case, as in many others, the supernormal is only normal after all.

Jeanne Dixon Predicts the Kennedy Assassination. On May 13, 1956, *Parade* magazine reported the amazing predictions of psychic Jeanne Dixon: "As to the 1960 election, Mrs. Dixon thinks it will be dominated by labor and won by a Democrat. But he will be assassinated or die in office, though not necessarily in his first term" (Kole 1984, 67).

Although this prediction has been heralded as a notable example of supernormal powers, it is really a classic example of vagueness that in retrospect looks like accuracy. First, her chances that a Democrat would be elected were fifty-fifty. Further, the presidents elected every twenty years since 1840 have died in office. And she had eight years (two terms) for her prophecy to be fulfilled. So her prediction was not so spectacular after all.

The untold failures of psychic predictions need to be weighed in the balance. Here are just a few of Jeanne Dixon's numerous predictions that have *not* come true (see Kole 1984, 70).

1. Russia would be first with men on the moon.
2. World War III would start in 1954.
3. The Vietnam War would end in 1966. (It ended in 1975.)
4. On October 19, 1968, she predicted that Jacqueline Kennedy was not contemplating marriage. (She married Aristotle Onassis the next day!)
5. She predicted that Castro would be overthrown in 1970. (He is still there.)

Professor F. K. Donnelly of the University of New Brunswick reviewed the predictions made by twenty-five psychics in *The People's Almanac* (1975), including Jeanne Dixon, Irene Hughes, and many others. The findings: "Out of the total 72 predictions, 66 (or 92 percent) were dead wrong" (Kole 1984, 69). It obviously does not take supernatural powers to accomplish these subnormal results.

It is perhaps incorrect to label such people as outright frauds, since it is possible they actually believe in their ability to predict future events. However, in the occasions (apparently rare, according to Professor Brunswick's findings) where the psychics were correct in their predictions, there is almost certainly nothing supernatural at work. Rather, using what is probably mere common sense, they occasionally guess correctly. What is merely a quirk—getting a few predictions right now and then—is hardly miraculous.

Supernormal Precognition. There are numerous cases on record of people who had a premonition of an event, such as the death of a loved one. But here, too, the evidence is often lacking that this has a supernormal cause. Take the case of Ray Hyman who said, "My brother was killed in World War II and my mother had a dream about it the night before it happened" (cited by Kole 1984, 38).

Luis Alvarez of the University of California offers a statistical explanation of such events. Such events should occur about ten times per day around the United States. "With such a large sample to draw from, it is not surprising that some exceedingly astonishing coincidences are reported in the parapsychological literature as proof of extrasensory perception in one form or another" (Kole 1984, 38).

Some psychologists offer an even more convincing explanation. As to the death of his brother in World War II, it is suggested that his mother, sister, and he all had dreams many times that their brother was killed. They just do not remember them because nothing happened to make them true. This fits with a current theory of memory—that we tend to remember things we can connect to something meaningful (Kole 1984, 38-39).

Fire Walking. With the increasing popularity of Eastern religions, fire walking has become almost a pastime for some. Here again there is a claim to spiritual powers by the gurus. Workshops on fire walking are now held around the country. Those who learn to accomplish this feat often believe they can do almost anything.

But are a few quick steps over several feet of hot coals really an evidence of supernatural power? Actual research has shown that the feat can be explained by purely natural laws. First of all, the coals are not as hot as one would suppose. (It is interesting to note that fire walkers do not walk on hot *metal.*) In fact, coals are a poor conductor of heat. They contain little heat energy because they are not massive.

Second, if the feet move quickly the coals do not have enough time to burn the skin. Since the coal is a poor conductor, the heat moves slowly and the foot is moved before it is burned. Third, in places where people go barefoot and have developed a protective sole on their foot, it is not very impressive at all to walk on hot coals. In short, there are perfectly good scientific explanations for fire walking.

Classifying the Unusual

Not everything unusual has a supernatural cause. In fact, there are many kinds of unusual events that can be mistaken for the miraculous by the untrained observer.

1. Seldom occurring but purely natural events

Eclipses, meteors, and earthquakes do not occur as regularly as other natural events, but they are not supernatural. They do have an observable pattern and can be predicted when the proper factors are known. Further, natural events can be repeated in a laboratory simulation, thus showing they can be done by purely natural means.

2. Natural coincidences

Sometimes the intersection of purely natural processes produces a highly unusual effect. The "northern lights" (aurora borealis) are an example of this. Several times people have reported fish raining from the sky. This is possible if a tornadolike wind sucked them out of the lake or sea and then gravity deposited them on the land. But these are only natural laws at work in an unusual way.

3. Mind-over-matter

The effects of the mind on the body are greater than many people believe. Many illnesses are known to have psychological causes. There have been many mental healings of certain kinds of diseases reported. Norman Cousins was healed of cancer by laughing (Cousins 1979). "Laugh therapy" is known to have positive physical effects (see Proverbs 17:22). One psychiatrist, Dr. Paul Meier, reported to me in 1987 of healing a girl of psychologically induced blindness with the power of suggestion.

4. Statistical oddities

Many unusual events are merely statistical oddities. Why have presidents elected every twenty years since 1840 died in office? It is probably just a statistical oddity. A little reflection, however, will show that many perfectly natural occurrences are statistically improbable. What are the chances that a pilot ejected from a burning plane at ten thousand feet with a burned chute would live to tell the story? They are statistically rare, but it did happen to Thomas Smoke over Little Rock, Arkansas, on March 31, 1960. In fact, the chances for a perfect bridge hand are only 1 in 635,013,559,600. But it has happened. Should we assume the dealer had supernormal powers?

5. Mirages

Most people have seen what looks like water on the road

ahead on a hot day, only to find that it disappears as they approach it. This same optical illusion has been seen at sea or in the desert. But, unusual as it is, it is a purely natural phenomenon.

6. The unexplained

There are many unusual natural events for which there is presently no good explanation. However, the unexplained is not necessarily unexplainable. Many things once mysteries are now general knowledge. No doubt many present mysteries will yield to natural explanation. Science has its anomalies (from *anomos*, "no law") which cannot be explained by any known scientific laws. But can we presume to know all that is knowable? Some things are simply unexplained; we just do not know what the cause is. But ignorance does not prove it was a miracle. Ignorance proves only ignorance. From nothing you can prove nothing.

Many cases of cancer go into spontaneous remission. The former president of the American College of Surgeons (*Spontaneous Regression of Cancer*) studied 176 such cases. However, as Dr. Paul Brand noted, "The remissions occur among Christians and non-Christians, with prayer and without prayer, and they represent only a very small percentage of the people with cancer who have been prayed for" (Brand 1983, 18).

Summary

There are many unusual things that occur. Some are miracles (see chapter 3), some are magic (see chapter 5), but some are just odd. That is, they have purely natural causes, even if they are unknown to us. In time these mysteries tend to yield to natural explanations. Meanwhile, there are certain earmarks of these unusual events.

1. Events that occur repeatedly but have no known cause. (What occurs repeatedly is a natural event.)
2. Events that can be repeated by purely natural means. (What is repeatable by natural means has a natural cause.)
3. Events that can be explained by mental causes. (Mental causes are not supernatural.)
4. Events with known possible causes but are statistical rarities. (Statistical rarities occur by purely natural causes.)

5. Events that can be duplicated by magicians using no supernormal powers. (What can be done naturally needs no supernatural cause.)
6. Events that we can be taught to do. (What can be taught is natural, not supernatural.)

Of course, in addition to these physically and mentally explainable occurrences, there are also demonically caused events (see chapter 7). But all of them fall short of being true miracles, as defined in chapter 2.

In brief, much of what passes as supernatural is merely natural. We must not assume from this, however, that apart from true miracles all unusual events have purely physical or mental causes. Simply because many unusual occurrences can be accounted for in this manner does not mean that all similar events can be so explained. We must guard against the fallacy of assuming that all such events have purely physical explanations. There are spiritual beings, good and evil, that can cause highly unusual events (see chapter 7). These satanically caused events the Bible calls "counterfeit miracles, signs and wonders" (2 Thessalonians 2:9).

However, much that passes for supernatural or supernormal is purely natural. The vast majority of unusual events have purely natural causes. Simply because someone attaches religious significance to them does not prove they are supernatural. Not everything evil was caused by the Devil. Likewise, not everything odd is of God. Come to think of it, it is odd that anyone should believe that the odd points to God.

5. Miracle or Magic?
Learning to Discern Human Fraud

I saw it with my own eyes. So did about three hundred other faculty members and students at Trinity Evangelical Divinity School. David could see with a glass eye! I was teaching at the seminary at the time (1973). Like others, I was curious to hear the testimony of David's father, once a Christian radio broadcaster. Little David had injured his left eye. It was eventually removed by surgery and replaced with a glass eye in August 1968. The father trusted God for healing and prayed faithfully for three years for the restoration of his son's vision.

On July 6, 1971, David burst out of his bedroom and announced with excitement that he could see with his "bad eye." The father was elated. He shared with the chapel assembly that David was examined by physicians who confirmed that vision was restored, even though his eye and optic nerve were both surgically removed.

We all crowded into the chapel to hear David's story and to witness the miracle with our own eyes. Here is what we saw. David's glass eye was taken out of the socket and put in a pocket. The gory empty socket was proof enough that he had no real eye. Then a black blindfold was examined by a student in the audience and placed over David's eyes. Items were collected from the audience at random. With the patch over his good eye and the glass eye taken out, David began to read what was written on the notes and collected items from the audience. I remember hearing him read "University of Delaware" from a student's ring.

Everyone was amazed at this apparent miracle, and God was praised. No one present expressed disbelief. How could we? Seeing is believing. And we all saw with our own eyes that David could see without his eye.

In spite of an uncomfortable feeling about the odd nature of this event, I have often shared it with others as a miracle that I personally witnessed. When challenged by skeptics, I have told them what I saw with my own eyes. But was it really a miracle? While I believe miracles are possible, let me tell you why I now believe that I could have been deceived.

Magicians Speak Out

The word *magic* is used in two basically different ways, as an occult practice or as the art of illusion. As used in this chapter, magic refers to the art of deception. Professional magicians make their living by deceiving. They have done everything from making rabbits appear out of hats to causing the Statue of Liberty to disappear. Magician David Copperfield made an airplane disappear off the runway. Some magicians can see even though they have a coin, clay, and blindfold over their eyes with bandages wrapped around their head. Yet they are doing it by trickery, not by supernatural power.

There is a perfectly natural explanation for what magicians do. Indeed, I now know how some of them do the eye trick. Anyone can do it with just a little practice and no special equipment. The performer puts an invisible lubricant on his cheek before the performance. Later, the clay, coin, and blindfold are placed over his eye. By lifting his forehead under the bandages, a small gap is made down the bridge of his nose through which he can see. The gig is up. It is not a miracle; it is magic.

Randi's Reward. Magician James Randi ("The Amazing Randi") has been carrying around a $10,000 check that he will give to anyone who demonstrates one supernormal feat under controlled conditions. So far he has not had to award a penny of it (Randi 1982, chapter 13).

"With all the claims of paranormal power that we see every day in the press," says Randi, "you'd think that I'd have many more people lined up to take the prize. As it stands, just fifty-two persons have passed the simple preliminaries, only to fail to support their claims to supernatural powers" (Kole 1984, 22).

Houdini's Challenge. The world-famous magician Harry Houdini exposed many fraudulent mediums. He had a standing challenge that he could duplicate by purely normal powers anything a spiritualist could do by their so-called supernormal powers. He spent years of research and attended some five thousand seances. After his mother's death he tried to communicate with her to find out what she uttered in her dying words to him that he could not hear. In many seances he heard ghostly voices whisper words purporting to be from his mother. The only problem was that the words were always in English and his mother spoke only Yiddish!

In his book, *A Magician among the Spirits,* Houdini declared,

I have never been baffled in the least by what I have seen at seances. Everything I have seen has been merely a form of mystification. The secret of all such performances is to catch the mind off guard, and the moment after, it has been surprised to follow up with something else that carries the intelligence along with the performer. (Quoted in Kole 1984, 56)

Uri Geller's Spoon-bending Powers. One of the most publicized powers is that of the Israeli-born Uri Geller. Millions have seen him bend spoons without touching them before their very eyes on national television. However, magicians are not so easily deceived by Geller. They are quick to note these things: 1) He rarely announces his intention to bend a spoon in advance. 2) In a controlled setting, when asked to bend a specific spoon without touching it, his powers mysteriously disappear. 3) He studied magic as a lad in Israel.

(Other magicians can do the spoon bending trick, too.)

Professor Persi Diaconis of Stanford University told about his experience with Geller.

Diaconis drove Geller to the airport after he had appeared at Stanford. While waiting for his flight, the psychic expressed disappointment that the professor remained a skeptic, and he offered to provide conclusive proof of his powers. He then asked Diaconis to reach into his coat pocket, grab his keys, and concentrate on a key that could be bent. The professor says, "I opened my hand and the key I was thinking of was bent. For about five minutes I was as badly fooled as I've ever been in my life." (Kole 1984, 28)

Diaconis eventually solved the mystery by rethinking what had happened on the trip to the airport. On the way Geller had insisted on sitting in the backseat where Diaconis's coat was. Later, at the airport, Geller insisted on bringing the coat in case it got cold. Only one of the four keys was bent, the one that could be bent easily. Further, Diaconis later found that Geller had also bent and twisted each of his pens in the coat. Geller had apparently prepared several objects that could later be used as "proofs" of his powers.

I personally saw Geller's powers fail to identify which can contained the key on the "Tonight Show" when Johnny Carson (also a magician) would not let him touch the table. Jarring it only a little could have revealed a slight sound from the can with the key.

Even the editors of the articles on the Geller experiments published in *Nature* magazine expressed concern over the scientific validity of the published results, saying the safeguards against fraud were "uncomfortably vague." Thus, "this in itself might be sufficient to raise doubt that the experiments have demonstrated the existence of a new channel of communication which does not involve the use of the senses" (Kole 1984, 27).

One researcher concluded that Geller's most sensational experiment was inconclusive. Geller correctly called the roll of a die in a steel box. But Gardner points out that Geller could have cheated in many ways. The only way to rule out the possibility of trickery would have been to have a knowledgeable magician present, or to see a videotape of all the attempts. "In the absence of such controls for guarding against deception by a known charlatan, the die test was far too casual and slipshod to deserve being included in a technical paper for a journal as reputable as *Nature*" (quoted in Kole 1984, 27).

Other magicians do similar tricks by purely natural powers. So there is no reason to believe Geller does his feats by supernatural power.

Healers with Special "Revelations." Several noted televangelists demonstrate seemingly extraordinary knowledge of those they heal, sometimes calling out the names, addresses, and particulars of the lives of those they heal. Three of these evangelists were researched by "Amazing Randi" and his team. They arrived early at the meetings and discovered that their wives and other "front men" were walking through the crowd and collecting information by informal conversations, which were relayed to the evangelist. They discovered that evangelist David Paul kept the information on small slips of paper in his Bible. On the paper was the name, disease, doctor, and sometimes an address. They reported that former employees of Paul said these slips were burned after the meeting.

Peter Popoff made use of modern technology to perform his "miracles." A small radio receiver was inserted in his left ear. His wife would transmit information to him from a concealed location. When asked by a Los Angeles television reporter why he employed this method, Popoff replied that he "was told to use this technique by the Holy Spirit" (Larue 1986, 46). Randi was able to record the radio transmission (which was later played on the "Tonight Show"). The recording revealed that every one of Popoff's miraculous "revelations" was fed to him by his wife. Randi later quipped, "Now we know that God has a female voice and that it sounds very much like Popoff's wife's voice!"

The case of evangelist W. V. Grant is equally illuminating. Randi and his associates observed many people with serious illnesses in wheelchairs in the auditorium. However, none of these ever got to Grant. Instead, Grant commanded several people to get up and walk from their wheelchairs. When Randi followed up on those who were "healed," he discovered that some were total fabrications, others were never healed, and some were not crippled to begin with (Kole 1984, 167-168). Independent research revealed that Grant's assistant would enlist some people who walked into the meetings to sit in a provided wheelchair until Grant asked them to stand. This kind of performance takes much less than supernatural power to accomplish its results.

Christian Magicians and the Paranormal. Many magicians can duplicate events considered to be paranormal. Several outstanding Christian magicians regularly perform feats by mere trickery that others claim to be supernormal. The famous Christian illusionist Andre Kole appears to read minds, to levitate, to make huge objects vanish in midair and to reappear from nowhere. Yet he reminds his audiences that "all my feats, though perhaps appearing supernatural, are accomplished by natural means" (Kole 1984, 13).

Another Christian illusionist, Danny Korem, performs the same kind of unusual feats and also admits they are done by purely normal powers. In 1979 he set the world's record by escaping from 1680 feet of rope (five times as long as a football field). He, too, sees most of the claims to perform supernormal feats as mere magical tricks (see Korem 1981).

Magician Danny Korem Exposes Frauds. Danny Korem has exposed a number of claims for supernatural powers as mere magical tricks. In his film *Psychic Confession*, Korem exposed a famous psychic, James Hydrick, who claimed mental powers to move an object beneath an overturned fish tank on a table. Korem demonstrated that the trick was being done by quietly breathing air on the table. The air moved under the tank and turned the fan wheel inside. On being exposed, the "psychic" confessed his fraud on camera. No miracle was involved; it was simply a magical trick.

In his book *The Fakers*, Korem exposes many other deceptions that often pass for supernormal powers. The art of "cold reading" is the ability to extract information from someone without their being aware. Korem tells "how the entertainer recognizes certain muscle reactions of the participants which, through experience, enable him to locate hidden objects" (Korem 1981, 104).

Coauthor and psychiatrist, Dr. Paul Meier, tells how the trained psychiatrist can identify many sensory clues to provide him with information concerning his patient. "It is the application of these same principles which enables the fortune-teller to divulge information to the subject that seemingly is impossible to perceive" (Korem 1981, 104).

Korem reveals the tricks of the trade: "Given the proper circumstances, anyone can be made to believe he has witnessed something which never took place" (Korem 1981, 19). The trick is that the magician (or deceiver) "must first fool the mind and then fool the eye" (Korem 1981, 19). Magic is divided into three levels: the *puzzler* that fools only the eye; the *fooler* where both eye and mind are deceived; and the *baffler* where the mind is fooled but not the eye (Korem 1981, 19).

Trickery is expected from magicians. What is tragic is when religious leaders use trickery to deceive their followers into believing they have miraculous powers. Jim Jones is a case in point. "People who 'died' and were revived 'miraculously' in the service were Jones's close associates in elaborate disguise, each one new for the occasion" (White 1979, 42). These farces were so carefully contrived that even Jones's photographer, Al Mills, and Tim Stoen, the second in command, did not realize they were faked (White 1979, 42). It was later discovered that Jones's bus was filled with makeup, wigs, crutches, and fake cancers. Researcher Mel White stated, "The people needed hope and healing. Through his so-called miracles he gave them both. And the people gave him money and power in return" (White 1979, 43).

Illusionist Andre Kole Speaks Out. In a very helpful book, *Miracle or Magic*, Christian illusionist Andre Kole reveals that many so-called miracles are really only magic. Take communication with the dead as an example. In 1848 the famous Fox sisters of Hydesville, New York, received answers from the spirits in distinct raps, apparently on the wall. People from all over the country came to observe this remarkable phenomenon. For forty years the Fox sisters made a great deal of money traveling throughout the country, demonstrating their powers.

On September 24, 1888, the *New York Herald* published a confession of the sisters which said, "As far as spirits were concerned neither my sister nor I thought about it. I knew there was no such thing as the departed returning to this life. I have seen so much miserable deception that every morning of my life I have it before me" (cited by Kole 1984, 54).

What about the knocking? They had accomplished it by snapping the joints of their toes, using the wooden floor as a sounding board. So much for their supernormal powers.

Andre Kole tells of his experience with a psychic surgeon in the Philippines. After reading Psalm 23, the surgeon prayed. Then he swabbed a woman's skin with a cotton ball. Blood appeared. He then plunged his hand into her abdomen and pulled out a piece of diseased tissue. He dropped it into a bucket by the table. He swabbed the skin and observers could see no incision. The woman was covered with a sheet and helped to her feet (Kole 1984, 9-10). There was no evidence of an incision. The woman was encouraged to read her Bible. She walked away.

Was this a miracle? No, it was actually a cunning deception. As a trained magician, Kole points out that

> it didn't take long to discover that the doctor used a very clever form of sleight of hand. The cut that his finger seemed to make actually was done with a small razor blade concealed in the healer's fingers. He concealed in his other hand the supposed diseased tissue, before apparently pulling it from the patient's body. . . . They performed their fake operations using some of the most clever sleight of hand that I ever have seen. Their incredible dexterity immediately reminded me of the ability of Ben Chavez, a Filipino magician with nimble fingers and a quality of manual dexterity almost unequaled in the magic world. (Kole 1984, 42-43)

Further investigation revealed that no incision was made. The surgeon used coagulated animal blood from his refrigerator. Others use red dye from betel nuts. The removed organs were not human but were tissue or parts from chickens, goats, or cows. It was not a miracle at all, just clever magic. But a lot of people have been fooled. What is tragic is that many people "cured" in this way have serious diseases that later need urgent attention by a real physician. Even more tragic are the people who never get the proper attention and eventually die as a result.

What about psychic mind-reading predictions? Here, too, in most cases there is nothing supernatural. Magicians, like Andre Kole, do the same thing all the time. Various techniques are used, including reading body language, probability projections, and inside information. One magician I know would go into the men's room before an act, sit in a stall with his feet up and listen to conversations that he would identify with the legs and shoes he could see. Later in the show, he was able to come up with some startling revelations about the people present.

Andre Kole tells how he was able to amaze a West Coast audience with his accurate prediction of J. R.'s shooting on the "Dallas" TV program. Even the actors on the show were not sure, since they had filmed several possible endings. But using a staff member on a long distance line to the East Coast (where the program aired earlier), he was able to learn hours in advance who shot J. R. So much for the amazing "prediction."

The fact that so-called psychics are sometimes (even often) wrong reveals that they are not true prophets of God. For one of the tests of a prophet is whether he ever gives a false prophecy. For God cannot be wrong. Hence, if a prophet claims to get a revelation from God and his prediction is wrong, then we know he (or she) is not a prophet of God. Moses wrote:

You may say to yourselves, "How can we know when a message has not been spoken by the Lord?" If what a prophet proclaims in the name of the Lord does not take place or come true, that is a message the Lord has not spoken. That prophet has spoken presumptuously.
(Deuteronomy 18:21-22)

How People Are Deceived

Magicians deceive people all the time. Magic is the art of deception. We even pay to be entertained by their illusions. Unfortunately there is evidence to demonstrate that there are religious frauds as well. Christians are also "paying" for these as well. Only the cost is not currency but credibility. Thank God for the professional Christian magicians who are exposing the fraudulent claims to supernormal powers. There is a big difference between miracle and magic. It is interesting to note that the Bible denotes the practitioners of false signs as "magicians" (see Exodus 7:11). For whether in its human or occult form, magic involves deception.

There is a clear distinction between the truly supernatural and the purely magical, between truth and trickery. Why, then, are so many people deceived? Here again the best insights come from those trained in the tricks of the trade—magicians.

Andre Kole's Four Reasons for Deception. According to Kole, there are four basic reasons why people are misled to believe that supernormal powers have been exercised (Kole 1984, 16).

First, the media blows many stories out of proportion. This is understandable; the sensational makes better reading and sells more copies. Often the headlines (intended as eye-catchers) claim more than the articles actually deliver. But even the articles themselves often overstate the case to keep the readers' attention. The problem with popular reporting is not only factual accuracy; it is also oversensationalizing. For example, I testified as an expert witness on philosophy, religion, and their borders with science at the famous "Scopes II" trial in Little Rock, Arkansas (December, 1981). The *Washington Post* story about my testimony read:

Creationist Tells of Belief in UFOs, Satan, Occult
Little Rock, Dec. 11—

The defense of the Arkansas creation law opened today with a spectacular courtroom fireworks display as the opening creationist witness described, under cross-

*examination, his belief in unidentified flying objects,
demon possession and the occult, which he said he sees as
actual satanic attacks in the world.*

As a matter of fact, there was nothing at all spectacular
about it. It was a rather long, deep, and almost dull two-hour
philosophical testimony on the nature of religion and science. Furthermore, my prepared testimony had nothing to
say about Satan or UFOs. That was brought in by the American Civil Liberties Union attorney at the last moment (over
objections by our lawyers) with the result that creationist
views were made to look ridiculous. The press took it from
there and created a sensation that did not exist (see Geisler
1982, 118, 127-129).

The *New York Times* got so carried away with creating the
sensation that they did not even hear the testimony correctly. They reported that I "believed in unidentified flying
objects as 'Satan manifestations for the purposes of deception.'" They added that "an article in *Reader's Digest* has
confirmed their existence." This exaggerated kind of reporting misleads even some otherwise careful scholars.

Dr. Langdon Gilkey, professor at the University of Chicago
Divinity School (and also a witness for the ACLU against
creation), gleefully accepted this *New York Times* article as
true. He wrote, "Needless to say, I was elated later when,
unable to hear Geisler's testimony at the trial, I read [it] in the
New York Times of December 12" (Gilkey 1985, 77). Gilkey's
book will be read by thousands of people who will accept it
as accurate because of his academic credentials.

However, the report was exaggerated, misleading, and
false. This is evident from several facts. First, the official
court record verifies that it was not the popular *Reader's
Digest* that was cited but the testimony of many scientists
(mostly evolutionists) taken from the *Science Digest* (November 1981). Furthermore, there was no audible "courtroom laughter" as was mentioned in the article. I talked with
some of the eyewitnesses present, and not one of them heard
any audible laughter. At best there may have been some quiet
snickering, probably by the reporter who wrote the story.
Finally, the topic of UFOs and Satan was not brought up by

me but by the ACLU attorney (in cross-examination) in order to discredit the creationist case. It worked. People have been deceived by their propaganda against creationist views. The same kind of misleading reporting is also true of newspaper accounts about supernormal events. They like to sensationalize.

Second, determination of the facts is often difficult. One of the difficulties in evaluating reports of unusual occurrences is that only certain facts are selected and unfavorable ones are omitted. Other reports are exaggerated, and in some cases the reports are actually fabricated. This is even true of usual phenomena, as the above discussion of my testimony at "Scopes II" illustrates. Kole uses the illustration of the famous magician, David Copperfield, who made a small Lear jet disappear from a runway. He says, "But I've heard people say he made a 747 jet disappear while it was flying through the air" (Kole 1984, 18)!

Another firsthand example of this second reason for deception is the testimony of an expert scientific witness for creation in Arkansas. Dr. Donald Chittick's testimony was discredited by news reports as follows:

But one witness confirmed he was a member of the Bible Science Association, which says putting "Christ and the Bible and the power of the Holy Spirit back into science is one of the most powerful methods of witnessing in the church today." (Arkansas Democrat, December 16, 1981)

Now, the distinct impression left by this is that Chittick is a wild-eyed religious zealot who wanted religious evangelism to go on in public schools. This impression is created by factual omission and distortion in the news report. Consider the following factors (omitted by the article) and notice how the impression changes.

1. Dr. Chittick has a Ph.D. in chemistry.
2. He was recognized by both the court and the ACLU as an "expert witness."
3. It was acknowledged by the ACLU and court that, using a creationist model, he had invented a fossil fuel that could

power a car at a fraction of the price of gasoline.
4. His answer to the question as to whether he agreed that he wanted to get religion back into the classroom was "No!"
5. It was not Dr. Chittick who had made that statement but someone else in the "Bible Science" organization who had written that letter.
6. The statement was brought up by the ACLU, not by Chittick, who repudiated it.

In spite of all this, the news report made it look like Chittick was a wild-eyed religious zealot bent on evangelizing public school science classes. When one sees how a news reporter's omission and distortion can leave the reversed impression of the truth, it is easy to see how exaggerated and false claims of the supernatural are created.

Third, when it comes to claims for the paranormal, science has difficulty discerning between fake and real (Kole 1984, 19). There are many reasons for this. First of all, these events usually are not done under controlled conditions. Further, the scientists often did not observe the event themselves. They have only second-hand, hear-say evidence. Finally, scientists are easy to fool because they do not expect a trick. Noted Christian magician, Danny Korem, wrote, "The best person to detect a trick is an expert in trickery—not a scientist" (Korem 1981, 18).

It is interesting to note that the alleged supernormal powers of psychics decrease as the controls are increased. The same is true of faith healers. Oral Robert's claims to have raised the dead moderated as reporters asked for names and addresses. When pressed to give reporters examples, he mentioned the instance of a girl who had apparently fainted in a service. His evidence that she was dead was that she was unconscious, her body felt cold, and both the mother and Oral Roberts believed she was dead. This is not credible evidence of a real physical death, to say the least.

Reports of raising the dead came out of the Indonesia revival reported in 1971. Mel Tari tells of people who were "raised from the dead" in his book, *A Mighty Wind*. However, when George Peters later went to Indonesia and carefully sifted through the evidence he concluded: "I do not doubt that God is able to raise the dead, but I seriously question that He did so in Timor [Indonesia]. In fact, I am convinced that it did not happen" (Peters 1973, 88).

Professor Peters interviewed people who were allegedly once dead and others who claimed to have raised the dead. He discovered several things. First, "their word for death may mean unconsciousness, coma, or actual death" (Peters 1973, 89). Second, he found that death in that culture was believed to be in three stages. In the first stage the soul is still in the body. In the second stage the soul is in the home or community. And in stage three the soul goes to the spirit world in the regions beyond. But "not one of the dead persons believed his soul had completely departed to the region beyond" (Peters, 89). So in the Christian concept of death (as the soul leaving the body and going to the spiritual world) none of these people had really died. Third, many of the people who claimed to have died could hear people in the room near their body. Others admitted they were not "totally dead" (Peters, 89).

It is obvious from the evidence uncovered by Peters that these people were not really physically raised from the dead but were only reawakened from a comalike state. They went from unconscious to conscious states, not from death to life.

Fourth, people deeply desire to see and believe supernormal phenomena (Kole 1984, 20). This eagerness to see the sensational and know the unknown obscures their rational judgment about alleged paranormal events. People become less critical when the emotional stakes are higher. For example, one's desire to communicate with a departed loved one could very easily blur his rational judgment about the evidence that the medium was really getting the information from the departed rather than from normal sources (such as books, newspapers, or body language). When someone wants something to be true, his will gets ahead of his mind.

Sigmund Freud spoke of this phenomenon as an "illusion," which he defined as something "derived from human wishes." He wrote:

Thus we call a belief an illusion when a wish-fulfillment is a prominent factor in its motivation, and in doing so we

*disregard its relations to reality, just as the illusion itself
sets no store by verification. (Freud 1964, 48)*

It is this psychological predisposition to believe in the supernormal that misleads many in their analysis of purely natural
events.

How to Distinguish Miracle from Magic. Some events, of
course, have a demonic cause (see chapter 7). But assuming
for the moment that an unusual event is either a divine
miracle or human magic, how can we tell the difference? The
following chart reveals the distinctive difference.

MIRACLE	MAGIC
Under God's control	Under man's control
Done at God's will	Done at man's will
Not naturally repeatable	Naturally repeatable
No deception involved	Deception involved
Occurs in nature	Does not occur in nature
Fits into nature	Does not fit into nature
Unusual but not odd	Unusual and odd

Miracles are unique. A truly supernatural event is under
God's control. Hebrews 2:4 tells us that miracles were given
"according to *his will*" (emphasis added). Likewise, the miraculous gifts of the Holy Spirit, such as tongues and healing,
were given by God "just as he determines" (1 Corinthians
12:11). Indeed, it was not the prophet or apostle who performed the miracle but rather God who did it through them.
Even Jesus was "accredited by God . . . by miracles, wonders
and signs, which God did" (Acts 2:22). Magical tricks, by
contrast, are totally in the hands of the magician. He is in
control and can do tricks at his will.

Neither can miracles be repeated at will. They are naturally unrepeatable singularities (see chapter 3). They do not
occur regularly. If they did, they would not be miracles. Of
course, God has on occasion performed the same kind
of miracle again. Jesus multiplied loaves twice, once for five
thousand (Matthew 14:14-21) and once for four thousand

(Matthew 15:32-39). The Bible records several people being raised from the dead (see Matthew 9:18-19; Luke 7:11-15; John 11:17-44).

But miracles by nature do not occur regularly (see Appendix 4). They are naturally unrepeatable events. A prophet did not usually repeat the same miracle over and over. Moses, for example, did not have a repeat performance of the Red Sea sensation. Nor did Joshua do an encore on the sun standing still miracle. Magicians, on the other hand, can repeat their tricks over and over again.

Neither do humans control the conditions under which miracles occur. Moses certainly did not control the conditions of the great miracle God did through him. Nor did Elijah control the conditions surrounding God's intervention on Mount Carmel. And certainly Mary did not control the factors relating to her virgin conception. But magicians control the environment of their trick. Indeed, some kind of control is necessary to the deception. And deception is at the heart of magic. David Copperfield did not really make the Lear jet disappear. It only appeared to do so. Miracles, on the other hand, really occur. There is no deception involved.

Miracles take place in the real, objective, physical world. Whether it is a virgin birth, turning water to wine, or walking on water, miracles are real, objective events. They happen "out there" in the real world. When Jesus was raised from the dead, He left an empty space and grave clothes behind in an actual tomb. Magic, however, is not objective but subjective. Birds do not really appear out of thin air. They only seem to do so. Magic does not take place in nature but in the mind. The person is fooled into believing something happened that did not really occur.

There is another difference between miracle and magic. Magical events are odd; they do not really fit into nature. In nature rabbits do not come from inside hats but from inside mother rabbits. Coins do not appear out of thin air (even though the governments seem to think so!); they come from mints which get metal from mines.

Miracles, however, are not odd; they fit into nature. Jesus' miraculous conception resulted in a natural nine month pregnancy. He turned water into real wine. In fact, He did immediately what nature does gradually. In this sense His nature miracles involved a speeding up of natural processes. Even the resurrection of Christ is not contrary to nature but complementary to it. It is a rebirth of the natural and a fulfillment of the spiritual desire for immortality. Miracles fit into nature and even make it operate more naturally. As C. S. Lewis noted,

I contend that in all these miracles alike the incarnate God does suddenly and locally something that God has done or will do in general. Each miracle writes for us in small letters something that God has already written, or will write, in letters almost too large to be noticed, across the whole canvas of Nature. They focus at a particular point either God's actual, or His future, operations on the universe. (Lewis 1947, 140)

Magic, by contrast to miracle, is a misfit. It is odd but not of God. Magic is a square peg in a round hole. Miracles are the key that unlocks the mysteries of the origin, intervention and climax of the natural world.

Summary

Not every abnormal event is supernormal. Some have purely natural causes (as seen in chapter 4). And some unusual events have a psychological cause, not a supernatural cause (see chapter 6). Others are satanic, not divine (see chapter 7). But many are just magic, not miracle. Thanks to the work of both skeptical and Christian magicians we are able to see some of the reasons people have been deceived. These include the following:

1. Exaggerated and misleading reports.
2. Difficulty in determining the facts.
3. Difficulty in distinguishing fake from real instances of supernormal events.
4. Rational judgment is obscured by the desire to see and believe supernormal phenomena.

A miracle can be distinguished from magic in that a miracle is an unrepeated event under God's control that does not deceive but really occurs and fits into the natural world. Magic, on the other hand, is a repeatable act of deception under the control of the magician that does not really occur in or fit into the natural world.

6. Psychological or Supernatural?
Mind Cures and Divine Cures

One person's cancer vanished. Another was healed of blindness. Numerous other diseases were cured, including arthritis, lameness, and deafness. How did these amazing healings occur? Who performed them? For those who believe all healings are supernatural, the answers are disappointingly natural. All these are actually natural cures that occur frequently by the purely natural process of mind over matter. Psychiatrists do these kinds of things with no pretense to supernatural power.

Take the case of the blind girl. Noted psychiatrist Dr. Paul Meier revealed that he healed a young woman of blindness by merely instructing her to sleep in another room and, when she would awake, she would be able to see. The cure came, just as the doctor ordered. Her sight was restored by the power of suggestion. Other doctors have recorded cures of chronic diarrhea by prescribing nothing more than sugar pills, referred to as placebos. Accounts of severe skin disease and even lameness have also been cured by psychosomatic means.

Mind over Matter

Many incredible things have happened simply because of the power of suggestion. People have been made sick and hospitalized simply because a group of friends (doing an experiment) have suggested to them they were ill. They have been "cured" the same way—when the friends later suggested that they looked better.

The effect of the mind on the body is called psychosomatic (*psyche*, mind; *soma*, body). I have personally felt the impact of the mind on the body. A number of years ago I suffered from a bad allergy that responded only to a strong prescription drug that I took daily. Dust, grass, flowers—almost anything would cause me to sneeze.

One Sunday morning, while talking to a church leader before the service, I sneezed at the flowers near the pulpit where I was later to preach. I asked him if he would mind moving the flowers. His response was a shock to my psyche. In a kind but firm tone he said, "The flowers are plastic." Whatever physical aspect there may have been to my problem, I knew that a lot of it was simply in my mind. Over the next weeks I gradually weaned myself off the drug. It has been at least fifteen years now, and the allergic condition is gone. There was no prayer, no laying on of hands, and nothing supernatural. It was simply a case of mind over matter.

My wife, Barbara, also had a dramatic psychosomatic cure. I remember how excited we were when the doctor announced she was pregnant with our first child. A call to the would-be grandparents was in order and, of course, an announcement to the congregation of the little country church we served. But the joy of expectant parenthood was followed by the inevitable "morning sickness." My wife had already been pregnant for a couple months before she was tested, and yet she had not been sick at all during that time. So it occurred to me that her nausea and vomiting immediately after she tested positive could be psychosomatic. Apparently she was convinced. Because she never had a single day of "morning sickness" again, either for our oldest or for the other five children! The mind has a powerful influence over the body.

Scientific Documentation. Doctor Paul Brand gives the following examples that confirm the mind's power to heal the body.

The mind can effectively control pain. This can be accomplished by simple mental discipline or by "flooding the gates" of the nervous system with distracting noises or additional sensations (e.g., acupuncture). . . .

● In the placebo effect, faith in simple sugar pills stimulates the mind to control pain and even heal some disorders. In some experiments among those with terminal cancer, morphine was an effective painkiller in two-thirds of patients, but placebos were equally effective in half of those! The placebo tricks the mind into believing relief has come, and the body responds accordingly. . . .

● Through biofeedback, people can train themselves to direct bodily processes that previously were thought involuntary. They can control blood pressure, heart rate, brain waves, and even vary the temperature in their hands by as much as 14 degrees.

● Under hypnosis, 20 percent of patients can be induced to lose consciousness of pain so completely that they can undergo surgery without anesthetics. Some patients have even cured their own warts under hypnosis. The hypnotist suggests the idea, and the body performs a remarkable feat of skin renovation and construction, involving the cooperation of thousands of cells in a mental-directed process not otherwise attainable.

● In a false pregnancy, a woman believes so strongly in her pregnant condition that her mind directs an extraordinary sequence of activities: it increases hormone flow, enlarges breasts, suspends menstruation, induces morning sickness, and even prompts labor contractions. All this occurs even though there is no "physical cause"— that is, no fertilization and growing fetus inside. (Brand 1983, 19)

Dr. William Nolen explains that "the patient who suddenly discovers . . . that he can now move an arm or a leg that was previously paralyzed had that paralysis as a result of an emotional, not a physical disturbance." It is known that "neurotics and hysterics will frequently be relieved of their symptoms by the suggestions and ministrations of charismatic healers. It is in treating patients of this sort that healers claim their most dramatic triumphs" (Nolen 1974, 287). So "there is nothing miraculous about these cures. Psychiatrists, internists, G.P.'s, any M.D. who does psychiatric therapy, relieve thousands of such patients of their symptoms every year." But they do it by purely natural means, claiming no special supernatural powers.

It is commonly known in the medical field that up to 80 percent of disease is stress-related. Writing in the *Christian Medical Society Journal*, Kenneth Pelletier noted that "one standard medical text estimates that 50 to 80 percent of all diseases have their origin in stress" (Pelletier 1980, 8). These emotionally induced diseases can often be reversed by psychological therapy or "faith healings" where the proper mental attitude occasions the body experiencing a healing effect.

To God Be the Glory. Simply because there was no prayer, no religious fanfare, and no supernatural intervention does not mean God should not be credited with these psychosomatic cures. After all, God created the mind, with all its wonderful abilities, as well as the body with its curative powers. And it is God who has marvelously fitted them to aid one another. In fact, God heals in many ways.
1. Through natural physical processes that He has created (Psalm 139:14).
2. Through proper eating and drinking (1 Timothy 5:23).
3. Through good mental attitudes (Proverbs 17:22).
4. Through special divine intervention (John 9:6-7).

The psalmist said we are "fearfully and wonderfully made" (139:14). The body is, to a large degree, self-healing— or, rather, God has made it in such a way that He enables it to heal itself. The physician can stitch up a wound, but it is God who heals it. The doctor can set a bone, but God can cause it to grow back together. Likewise, the Bible recognizes the effect of the mind on one's health: "A cheerful heart is good medicine, but a crushed spirit dries up the bones" (Proverbs 17:22). In his book *Anatomy of an Illness*, Norman Cousins described in detail how he literally laughed himself well from cancer. Anyone who has thought about it knows the effect that bad news has on one's health. We can actually get sick when saddened by tragedy. Likewise, we can get well upon hearing good news. Few children are sick on Christmas morning, at least not psychosomatically sick.

Since God has created us as mind-body unities, He should get the credit when this marvelous relationship of mind affecting body is used to bring healing to our bodies. However, it is a serious overclaim to call these kinds of cures supernatural.

Some Things That the Mind Cannot Do. The mind cannot heal everything. There are some conditions "faith" cannot cure. We can name them but we cannot claim them. These are in the category of organic diseases. For example, the power of positive thinking cannot avoid death, raise the dead, see without eyes, grow amputated limbs, or restore those paralyzed by spinal injury. Dr. William Nolen explains, "Patients that go to a . . . service paralyzed from the waist down as a result of injury to the spinal cord, never have been and never will be cured through [faith-healing]" (Nolen 1974, 286).

Joni Eareckson Tada is a classic case in point. She became a quadriplegic as a result of a swimming accident. In spite of fervent prayers, she remains unhealed by all the faith she could muster. Joni concludes, God certainly can, and sometimes does, heal people in a miraculous way today. But the Bible does not teach that He will *always* heal those who come to Him in faith. He sovereignly reserves the right to heal or not to heal as He sees fit (Eareckson 1978, 132).

God Heals in Different Ways

God should be given the credit for all true healings, whether miraculous or natural, whether supernatural or psychological. After all, God is in control of both. Natural cures are simply the way God usually works, and miracles are the way He works on special occasions. Although the Bible speaks of demonic "signs" (see chapter 7), there is a question as to what extent demons can actually heal. Insofar as they have minds that can influence human minds they can no doubt heal in psychosomatic ways. On the other hand, being finite spirits their powers are limited, and they cannot give life or bring back the dead.

We do know, however, that demons can cause sickness. And when they withdraw (for whatever purpose), the normal divinely instituted processes by which health is restored take over. But God should be given the credit for this, not the devil. One thing seems to be evident in the demonic "healings," namely, the person is not really helped by them but is actually hooked by them. Satan never gives with the right hand without taking away more with the left hand. So while he appears to be delivering the person physically, he is really deceiving them spiritually.

Healing Through Natural Processes. Physicians know that they do not heal; the body does. Or, rather, God heals through the bodily processes He has set in operation. Dr. Brand summarized this well:

I see evidence of physical healing in the human body every day. Ironically, most patients visit a doctor because of healing, not disease: the symptoms that cause patients alarm are usually spectacular demonstrations of the body's healing mechanisms at work." (Brand 1983, 16)

For example, a doctor can set a bone, but only the body can heal the break. Likewise, a physician can make the needed incision, but only the body can repair it. In short, God is at His healing work through the bodily process that He has created. These kinds of healings are perfectly natural.

Nature does not operate apart from God. Nature is the way God works regularly, in a repeatable and predictable way. Without these regular laws of nature, life would not be possible. We must be able to count on the same predictable pattern of events or we could not walk, talk, or eat. Suppose, for example, that the law of gravity was not regular and predictable, but erratic and willy-nilly. If we could not depend on gravity, we could not even drink a glass of water without knowing whether it would go up our nose or down our throat.

God Also Heals in a Supernatural Way. Miracles, in contrast to natural healings, are the way God works on special occasions. They are not regular events but singular events. The way God heals regularly is slowly. But in a miracle God works immediately (see chapter 2). When Jesus healed the man with leprosy, He said, "'Be clean!' Immediately the leprosy left him and he was cured" (Mark 1:42). Likewise, when Jesus pronounced the woman well, "the woman was healed from that moment" (Matthew 9:22).

Many of Jesus' miracles involve a speeding up of a natural process.[1]

For example, wine is normally produced gradually when rain falls, is drawn up the grape vines, and formed into grapes, which then slowly ferment. Jesus, however, turned water into wine immediately. This was a miracle (John 2:11). Likewise, the farmer puts grain into the ground and it slowly multiplies into more grain by harvest time. Jesus, however, took bread (grain) and immediately multiplied it into more bread to feed five thousand men. This was a miracle (John 6:10-12).

Many people refer to the "miracle" of birth or the "miracle" of life. This is understandable, since God is the one who causes both. But it really confuses the issue to speak of natural, gradual, and repeatable events as "miracles." They are simply the way God works regularly. They are marvelous, but not miraculous.

By contrast with the way God usually operates, a true miracle is not a natural activity but a supernatural act. It is not the usual way God does it but a highly unusual way. This is why one of the biblical words for miracle is *wonder* (see Appendix 7). There is something wonderful, special, and unusual about a miracle. It attracts our attention. For instance, there is nothing unusual about a bush burning in a desert. But when it burns without being consumed and then the voice of God speaks from it, it is not a natural event (Exodus 3:1-14).

---

1. Of course, there is more to these miracles than merely speeding up a natural process. Divine intervention also involves the interjection of something else not previously there. Wine, for example, is constituted of more than mere water.

The question, then, is this: How do we distinguish a normal cure from a miraculous one? Or, more specifically, how can we tell a psychological cure from a supernatural one?

Faith Healing or Divine Healing?

Is faith necessary for a miracle? Can someone be healed, even if he does not believe he can be? If we are speaking of a true miracle, as defined above, then the answer is clearly yes. Jesus often performed miracles apart from belief that the miracle would happen.

There are thirty-five miracles of Jesus recorded in the Gospels (see Appendix 1). Of these, faith of the recipient is only exercised in ten of them:

1. Healing the lame man (John 5:1-9).
2. Cleansing a leper (Matthew 8:2-4).
3. Healing withered hand (Matthew 9:2-8).
4. Healing man born blind (John 9:1-7).
5. Healing blind Bartimaeus (Matthew 20:29-34).
6. Healing the hemorrhaging woman (Matthew 9:20-22; Mark 5:24-34; Luke 8:43-48).
7. Cleansing the ten lepers (Luke 17:11-19).
8. Peter walking on water (Matthew 14:24-33).
9. First miraculous catch of fish (Luke 5:1-11).
10. Second miraculous catch of fish (John 21:1-11).

In most of the cases where faith is present, it is not explicitly demanded as a condition for the miracle. Even in the few cases where faith is the condition for a miracle, it is probably faith in Jesus as Messiah that is required, not faith that the person could be healed. So even here faith is not required in order to be healed. Faith is not necessary for the healing, even though it may accompany it.

By contrast, the so-called faith movement today requires faith as a condition for the healing. Those who are not healed did not have enough faith. Those who get healed had faith. Faith becomes the psychological condition and conditioning for the healing. There is nothing miraculous about this. This can be accomplished without faith in Christ or the God of the Bible. Anyone who believes enough in anyone or anything can be healed this way. In fact, gurus and shamans perform the same kind of healings.

Miracles Where Faith Is Absent. In the vast majority of Jesus' miracles faith is not present at all, either explicitly or implicitly. This is true of at least eighteen of Jesus' miracles. In some cases the faith is a result of the miracle, not a condition of it. For example, when Jesus performed His first miracle (of turning water to wine), the Bible says, "He thus revealed his glory, and his disciples put their faith in him" (John 2:11).

Jesus' disciples did not believe He could feed the five thousand by multiplying loaves and fishes (Luke 9:13-14; Matthew 14:17). And even after they had seen Jesus feed five thousand, they disbelieved that the four thousand could be fed, saying, "Where could we get enough bread in this remote place to feed such a crowd?" (Matthew 15:33). In the case of the paralytic, Jesus healed him, not because of his faith, but only when He saw "their faith," that is, the four who carried him to Jesus (Mark 2:5).

Miracles Where Faith Could Not Have Been a Condition

There are seven miracles Jesus performed that could not have required faith by the recipient. This is certainly true of the three persons Jesus raised from the dead. No matter what implications can be read into other situations, there is no way dead corpses can believe. Yet Jesus raised Lazarus (John 11), the widow's son (Luke 7), and Jairus's daughter (Matthew 9).

Further, none of the nature miracles could have required faith in the recipient. This is true of the cursed fig tree (Matthew 21), the miracle of the tax money in the fish (Matthew 17:24-27), the two times Jesus multiplied loaves (Matthew 14; 15), and calming the sea (Matthew 8:18-27).

Neither can it be shown that faith of the disciples was required for these miracles to occur. In fact, in most cases it states that the disciples *lacked* faith. In the miracle of raising Lazarus Jesus prayed for those present "that they may believe" that God had sent Him (John 11:42). In the case of the first miraculous catch of fish, Peter expressed his unbelief, saying, "We've worked hard all night and haven't caught anything. But because you say so, I will let down the nets" (Luke 5:5). When to his surprise the nets came up full Peter "fell at Jesus' knees and said, 'Go away from me, Lord; I am a sinful man!'" (Luke 5:8). Just before Jesus rebuked the waves He said to the disciples, "Where is your faith?" (Luke 8:25). Even after He calmed the waters He said, "Do you still have no faith?" (Mark 4:40).

Miracles Where Disbelief Was Present. Sometimes Jesus performed miracles in spite of the unbelief of the people. The disciples lacked faith to cast the demon out of the boy (Matthew 17:14-21). Even the passage most often used to show that faith is necessary proves just the opposite. Matthew 13:58 tells us that "he did not do many miracles there because of their lack of faith." However, in spite of their unbelief in Him, Jesus did "lay his hands on a few sick people and heal them" (Mark 6:5).

But if Jesus healed some, even though there was no faith there, then belief is certainly not a condition of the miracle being performed. Even for what Jesus called "a wicked and adulterous generation" He offered the miracle of the Resurrection (Matthew 12:39-40). Indeed, Jesus appeared to His unbelieving brothers, James and Jude (1 Corinthians 15:6-7; see James 1:1; Jude 1). Likewise, Christ appeared to His unbelieving disciple, Thomas, saying, "Stop doubting and believe" (John 20:27).

The Dangers of Presumptive Faith

The devil tempted Jesus to leap from the pinnacle of the temple and trust God to save Him. Satan even quoted Scripture (out of context) to support his claims (Matthew 4:6). Jesus rebuked Satan by Scripture (in context), declaring, "Do not put the Lord your God to the test" (Matthew 4:7). One of the great dangers of "faith" healings is that one may have the faith but not the healing. While not all in the movement go this far, in fact many people have died believing that they were healed.

"We Let Our Son Die." One tragic example of this kind of presumptive faith is the case of Wesley Parker, whose parents believed that he was healed of diabetes and withdrew his insulin. When the symptoms persisted, they were encouraged to trust God that the disease was really gone; it was

simply the symptoms that persisted. They did, and the boy died. Still believing God, they proclaimed triumphantly that their son would rise from the dead. The boy is still dead.

The Parkers have since seen the error of such presumptive faith. They have confessed their sin in a book titled *We Let Our Son Die*. Listen to their tragic words as the judge found them guilty of involuntary manslaughter.

"Guilty . . . guilty . . . guilty. . . ." I glanced helplessly at the jury—some were quietly weeping, the others sitting solemnly. Accompanied by [Attorney] Russler, we entered the hallway and twisted our way through the maze of whirring cameras, glaring lights and shouting reporters. "What do you think of the verdict?" When we finally made it to his office and closed the door, I collapsed in the nearest chair—physically and emotionally drained. "Vultures!" Lucy [Parker] hissed. "They're nothing but a bunch of vultures." At that, she began to sob uncontrollably. . . . Unable to verbalize her agony, she wept uncontrollably until she felt released from her pent-up tensions. At home the next morning I stared at the headline in The Sun-Telegram: Parkers Found Guilty in Their Son's Death. (Parker 1980, 178-180)

West Coast charismatic pastor Chuck Smith reports, "I know of many people who have died while making their positive confessions of healing" (Smith 1983, 137). This is the sad tragedy of making a healing dependent on faith. We can "name it and claim it," but no amount of faith can make it happen. God is in control of us. Our faith does not control Him.

"His Flesh Shall Become as a Little Child's." Week after week I visited a neighbor who was dying of cancer. His body was jaundiced by the effects of the disease. Many times in his earlier life he had seen people raised from their beds of sickness after he prayed for them. Full of hope, he asked me to do the same for him. I mustered all the faith I could and called upon God, fearing in advance the guilt I would have if God did not come through.

There was no immediate restoration, but he seemed content to wait. In fact, a few days later his wife was jubilant. She triumphantly announced that God had assured her that her husband would be healed. "How do you know?" I asked expectantly. "God revealed to me," she said aglow, "while reading the Bible that my husband's 'flesh would become again as a little child's.'" "Oh," I said with heart sinking because of her misapplication of the passage. "That's wonderful, that's marvelous"; what else could I say.

I did not have the heart to rob this desperate lady of the blessing she experienced by giving her a lesson in proper Bible interpretation. Even though I knew this passage about the healing of Naaman the leper (2 Kings 5:14) was not meant for her husband, I held my silence. *Well*, I rationalized to myself, *maybe God sometimes blesses verses out of context. Maybe God has rewarded her faith, even in ignorance. Maybe my fears are unwarranted.* At any rate I did not want my unbelief to hinder her miracle. I too mustered all the faith I could to believe he would be healed. But doubts lingered, and I felt very much like the man who prayed, "Lord, I believe. Help thou my unbelief." Further, I could not get away from the fact that she was so sure. She even radiated with the joy of the Lord.

Eventually, however, my worst fears were realized; her husband died. As I returned to comfort her, I had no idea what to say. Faith had failed. And in my heart of hearts I knew why. It was not biblical faith; it was presumptive faith. It was not based on the actual meaning of any promise of God in Scripture. It was presumptive faith, grasping for support from Scripture by jerking statements out of context.

From Pulpit to Prison. "Indiana Grand Jury Indicts a Faith-Healing Preacher." So went the headline (*Christianity Today*, 23 November 1984). Hobart Freeman of Faith Assembly taught that "to seek medical care demonstrates a lack of faith in God's ability or desire to heal the body supernaturally." The result: eighty people, many of whom were children, died. The grand jury indicted Freeman on charges of aiding and inducing reckless homicide. One member of Freeman's church, fifteen-year-old Pamela, died of chronic kidney failure, a condition that was medically treatable. Her parents were the third of Faith Assembly couples to be indicted in four months. The others were convicted. The Indiana Circuit Court judge sentenced Gary and Margaret Hall to five years in prison. They were found guilty of criminal negligence of their twenty-six-day-old son, who died of pneumonia. As for pastor Freeman, he boasted that since he received "the baptism of the Holy Spirit" in 1966, "I have not spent a dime on medicine or medical care." He died a short time later of heart failure (Lawson 1985, 110).

How to Tell the Real Thing

There is a clear distinction between psychological and supernatural healing. Anyone who knows the facts of the case can spot the real thing. A truly miraculous cure is distinguished from a mental one by the following characteristics.

Miracles Do Not Require Faith of the Recipient. God is in sovereign control of the universe, and He can and does perform miracles with or without our faith. Miracles are done "according to his will" (Hebrews 2:4). Miraculous gifts were distributed to New Testament believers "according to his will" (1 Corinthians 12:11). And as the above discussion of His miracles revealed, Jesus performed miracles where there was no faith and even where there was unbelief.

On the other hand, psychological healings require faith on the part of the recipient. Those who suffer from psychosomatic illnesses must believe they can be cured. Whether they believe it is God, a physician, or an evangelist—they must believe to be healed. In fact, it is their faith that makes the healing possible. But there is nothing supernatural about that kind of healing. It happens to Buddhists, Hindus, Roman Catholics, Protestants, even atheists. Healers claiming supernatural powers can do it, but so can psychologists and psychiatrists by purely natural powers and placebo (sugar) pills.

Miracles Do Not Require Personal Contact. Sometimes the apostle laid hands on those whom God miraculously cured (Acts 8:18). However, it was not essential to the miracles, as is manifest from the fact that many whom Jesus never touched were healed. Jesus raised the nobleman's son from the dead from a long distance away (John 4:50-54).

Jesus never touched Lazarus when he brought him back to life (John 11:43-44). True, the apostle laid hands on the Samaritan believers so they could receive the Holy Spirit (Acts 8:18) and speak in tongues (Acts 19:6). Yet the apostles themselves received the Holy Spirit and tongues without anyone laying hands on them (Acts 2:1). Jesus performed many other healings for people who were not even present (John 4:49-53).

By contrast, many faith healings depend on the laying on of hands or some other physical contact or personal influence. Some healers use prayer cloths (see Appendix 6). Others ask listeners to place their hands on the radio. One evangelist asks people to stand on the Bible, with their hands on the TV. The personal contact or at least the psychological build up seem to be conditional to the healing itself. Not so with miracles that God performs. They occur without any physical contact or psychological build up. As mentioned above, many of Christ's miracles were performed without any faith of the recipient. A true miracle does not depend on human faith but on divine power.

Miracles Involve No Relapses. Biblical miracles lasted; there were no relapses. When Jesus healed a disease it did not return. Of course, everyone eventually died, even those He raised from the dead. But this was only as a result of the natural process of mortality, not because the miracle was canceled. Everyone eventually dies as a result of Adam's sin (Romans 5:12). And most people, even those who are healed, will get sick again. But this does not mean that the miracle was not lasting. It simply means that the body eventually yields to the effect of the Fall (Genesis 3:14-19; Romans 5:12; 8:18-22). Nonetheless, when Jesus performed a miracle, it lasted. Whatever other eventual problems the body had, it was not because that miracle did not immediately and permanently repair that problem.

On the other hand, psychological cures do not always last. This is true whether they are induced by hypnotism, placebo pills, or faith healers. In fact, not only those "healed" but also the healers have eventually succumbed to bad health. Faith healer Kathryn Kuhlman died of a chronic heart condition. Likewise, Hobart Freeman died prematurely with a cardiac condition. Charismatic pastor Chuck Smith wrote, "I also know that some of the evangelists who are the chief exponents of this positive confession as the way to constant health and continuous prosperity have spent time in the hospital for nervous exhaustion" (Smith 1983, 136-137).

Miracles Are Always Successful. Jesus never failed in any miracle He attempted. Indeed, since a miracle is an act of God, it is impossible for it to fail. For "with God all things are possible" (Matthew 19:26). It is true that Jesus did not always attempt to do a miracle. Sometimes He stated why (Matthew 13:58). Since He was not in the entertainment business, Jesus did not always satisfy the fancy of His audience. Nor did He "cast pearls before swine" (Matthew 7:6). God does miracles "according to his will" (Hebrews 2:4) and for His purposes, not for man's pleasure. But when God attempts a supernatural event, He is always successful.

Psychological attempts to heal are by no means 100 percent successful. In fact, there are many kinds of physical problems that are not curable by a patient's "faith." It has been known for some time that psychological cures are frequent on certain (suggestible) types of personality, such as the hysteric and the hypochondriac. Some studies show that the vast majority of people in the healing movement have these personality types.

Miracles Work on Organic, Not Just Functional, Illness. Jesus healed people born blind (John 9), and born lame (John 5). The apostles cured a man lame from birth (Acts 3:2). Jesus restored a withered hand immediately (Mark 3:1-5). He also performed miracles over nature, such as calming the wind (Matthew 8), walking on water (Mark 6), multiplying bread (John 6), and turning water into wine (John 2).

Psychological means cannot be used to bring about organic healings or miracles in nature. They are usually effective only on functional diseases. Most often they only aid or speed recovery. Never do they instantaneously produce a cure of incurable organic diseases or the restoration of limbs.

Dr. Brand stated flatly that he had "never yet heard an account of miraculous healing of pancreatic cancer or of cystic fibrosis, or of a major birth defect, or amputation" (Brand 1983, 18). George Bernard Shaw once caustically commented that the healings at Lourdes, France, left him unconvinced because he had seen many crutches and wheelchairs on display but not one glass eye, wooden leg, or toupee.

Miracles Are Always Immediate. As mentioned earlier, Jesus healed people "immediately" (Mark 1:42). When He spoke the sea was calmed "completely" (Matthew 8:26). Likewise, when the apostle healed the man lame from birth, "instantly the man's feet and ankles became strong" (Acts 3:7). Even in the one case of a two stage miracle, each stage was accomplished immediately (Mark 8:22-25). Miracles produced instantly what nature, at best, does only gradually (see chapter 2). And contrary to biblical miracles, when psychological healings do occur immediately, they are on functional and psychosomatic kinds of illnesses. The instantaneous cure of organic and incurable diseases as a result of calling upon God is a sign of a true miracle (see John 9:32).

Summary

The mind can aid in the healing process. A positive mental attitude often hastens the natural curative process. Further, when the sickness is psychologically caused, there can be a dramatic reversal when the person suddenly believes he can be healed. In this sense some psychosomatic and even demonic cures can be immediate. But they cannot be done on all diseases, especially organic and incurable kinds.

"Faith" cures of functional diseases are not supernatural for they lack the characteristics of a true miracle which are immediate on all kinds of diseases, including incurable ones (see chapter 2). Furthermore, healing occurs of believers and unbelievers as well, for those who believe in God, and those who don't. Faith healers can do it, but so can psychiatrists. It can be done by cults as well as Christians.

A true supernatural healing has distinctive earmarks. By contrast, a mere psychological healing does not have these unique features. The following chart summarizes the differences.

SUPERNATURAL HEALINGS	PSYCHOLOGICAL HEALINGS
Do not require faith	Require faith
Do not require physical contact	Often require personal contact
Are always successful	Are not always successful
Have no relapses	Have many relapses
Include all kinds of diseases (including organic ones)	Do not include all kinds of diseases (usually only functional ones)
Always immediate	Often not immediate

7. Demonic or Divine?
Satanic Marvels vs. Divine Wonders

While 94 percent of Americans believe in God, only 34 percent believe in a personal devil. The Devil has apparently been successful in concealing his existence, especially to the culturally "enlightened." C. S. Lewis revealed Satan's strategies when Screwtape, the under-secretary of the Devil, advised Wormwood, a junior demon missionary, on how to keep humans in ignorance of the devils' existence.

I wonder you should ask me whether it is essential to keep the patient in ignorance of your own existence. That question, at least for the present phase of the struggle, has been answered for us by the high command. Our policy, for the moment, is to conceal ourselves. Of course, this has not always been so. We are really faced with a cruel dilemma. When the humans disbelieve in our existence we lose all the pleasing results of direct terrorism. . . . On the other hand, when they believe in us, we cannot make them materialists and skeptics. At least, not yet. I have great hopes that we shall learn in due time how to emotionalize and mythologize their science to such an extent that what is, in effect, a belief in us (though not under that name) will creep in while the human mind remains closed to belief in the Enemy [God]. . . . But in the meantime we must obey our orders. I do not think you will have much difficulty in keeping the patient in the dark. The fact that "devils" are predominantly comic figures in the modern imagination will help you. (Lewis 1961, 32-33)

The Devil Is Alive and Evil . . .

Is the Devil for real? The Bible's answer to this question is unequivocal. It reveals his existence from the very beginning. He appears on earth as soon as humans do (Genesis 3) and reappears again and again to the very end (Job 1; Matthew 4; Revelation 20). We see the Devil's victory in the earliest chapters of Genesis. And his defeat is not complete until the very last chapters of Revelation (Revelation 20).

The Devil in Scripture. The Devil's first appearance in Scripture is as a subtle serpent who tempts Eve and precipitates man's fall into sin (Genesis 3:1f.). Later, it becomes clear that he has cohorts in his crime called "demons" (Deuteronomy 32:17) who lead men into idolatry, immorality (Leviticus 17:7), and even child sacrifice (Psalm 106:37). In fact, one-third of all the angels that God created followed Satan in his rebellion (Revelation 12:4). Over and over again in the Bible demons appear, sometimes to lie (1 Kings 22:21), often to encourage idolatry (Deuteronomy 32:17), and always in opposition to God's plan and people (Daniel 10:13-20).

In the New Testament the appearance of Christ on earth seems to stir the legions of darkness. Jesus gave His disciples special power over demons (Matthew 10:1). The apostles rebuked evil spirits for their work of divination (Acts 16:16-18). They cause sickness (Matthew 12:22-24) and produce violent seizures in some of their captives (Matthew 17:18). They are said to "possess" certain people (Matthew 12:22-24) and even speak from within them (Mark 5:8-9; Luke 4:33).

To the very end of time demons are active. In the Tribulation they are busy performing "signs" to deceive the kings of the earth (Revelation 16:14). During Christ's reign on earth the Devil and his angels are tied for "a thousand years" (Revelation 20:2). At the end of that period they are loosed only to deceive the nations once more before their final doom (Revelation 20:3).

Perhaps the most vivid account of the Devil is the temptation of Christ. In fact, Jesus carried on a conversation with the Devil, rebuking him three times with Scripture (Matthew 4:4, 7, 10). Nowhere is the reality of the Devil more evident in Scripture than in the intense battle between Christ and Satan. Of the twenty-nine references to Satan in the Gospels, twenty-five of them come from the lips of Christ.

The Devil Outside of Scripture. There are numerous indications outside of the Bible that demons are alive and active on planet earth. Several can be briefly cited here.
   1. *Evidence from pagan religions*
   Paul informs us that idolatry is demon-inspired. He wrote to the Corinthians, "Do I mean then that a sacrifice offered to an idol is anything, or that an idol is anything? No, but the sacrifices of pagans are offered to demons, not to God, and I do not want you to be participants with demons" (1 Corinthians 10:19-20). Pagan religions to this day sacrifice to demons. Their reality is obvious to any missionary who has worked in these countries. Indeed, paganism is on the rise in so-called civilized countries today, including Europe and America.
   2. *Evidence from occult activity*
   Moses warned the children of Israel:

When you enter the land the LORD your God is giving you, do not learn to imitate the detestable ways of the nations there. Let no one be found among you who sacrifices his son or daughter in the fire, who practices divination or sorcery, interprets omens, engages in witchcraft, or casts spells, or who is a medium or spiritist or who consults the dead. Anyone who does these things is detestable to the LORD. (Deuteronomy 18:9-12)

Today we refer to such mediums or spiritists as "channelers" or "psychics," but the Bible calls them demonic. Evidence is all around us that such mediums exist today as the instrument of demons.
   3. *Evidence from "out-of-body" experiences*
   The Bible says the soul leaves the body only once—at death (Hebrews 9:27; James 2:26). Once the soul leaves the body it goes to the next world (2 Corinthians 5:9) and cannot return (Luke 16:26). Hence, those who "experience" such

states are either hallucinating or being demonically influenced. Since many of these experiences are connected with demonic teaching and practice (1 Timothy 4:1f.), they offer further evidence of demonic activity.

4. *Evidence from attempted contacts with the dead*

The Bible forbids any attempt to contact the dead (Deuteronomy 18:11). While much fakery exists in these areas (see chapter 4), not all such activity is devoid of demonic influence. The practice of contacting the dead, known as "necromancy," has long been associated with evil spirits. They sometimes deceive those desiring to speak with a loved one by imitating his voice and relating information. The late Bishop Pike, who denied the deity of Christ, was apparently subjected to such an experience. He went to mediums who purported to give him messages from the bishop's departed son. He was deceived (Pike 1976).

The famous author of *Death and Dying*, Elisabeth Kubler-Ross, claims to have had many visitations from the dead. She was even encouraged to write her book, in which she claims that we need not fear death, by a former patient who returned from the dead (*Chicago Tribune*, 7 November 1976, Sect. 1, p. 24). Subsequently, she is reported to have had sexual intercourse with several "spirits" including one named "Salem" and another named "Willie." Since the devil has led the human race in the denial of death (Genesis 3:4) and into immoral practices (Jude 7), this is further evidence of demonic influence.

5. *Evidence from mediums and channelers*

Actress Shirley MacLaine has made a fad out of channeling. Her TV special in 1987 featured Kevin Ryerson, a medium who went into a trance on camera and conveyed "revelations" from a departed spirit. Edgar Cayce was one of the most famous mediums of our century. He provided untold "communications" from the world beyond. Cayce analyzed well his own source of information when in a sober moment he reflected as follows:

Against this I put the idea that the Devil might be tempting me to do his work by operating through me when I was conceited enough to think God had given me special power. . . . If ever the Devil was going to play a trick on me, this would be it. (Sugue 1973, 210)

6. *Evidence from "close encounters"*

Much talk about UFOs (Unidentified Flying Objects) actually pertains to IFO (Identified Flying Objects). Some people have not sighted UFOs but have simply seen the moon, meteors, or a light reflecting off a cloud. Other witnesses to UFOs have seen swamp gas, some a military aircraft, and still others have been hallucinating. However, not all UFOs can be so easily explained. There are many hard-core cases that defy usual explanations. Especially when they are encounters of "the third kind" involving ET (extraterrestrials).

Many scientists testify to having seen UFOs. Several years ago *Science Digest* carried an article entitled "Scientists Who Have Seen UFO's" (November 1981). It observed that some 10 percent of UFO sightings remain unexplained and that even "the late University of Colorado physics professor Edward U. Condon, a hard-nosed UFO skeptic, conceded that these sightings were 'indeed strange and mysterious, impossible by all current knowledge to explain.'"

Some of the data connected with UFO experiences parallels with the biblical teaching about demons. Consider the following:

● UFOs "materialize" from nowhere and vanish again into thin air just as angels did in the Bible (Genesis 18-19).

● Their flight patterns defy those of physical objects (e.g., making right turns at thousands of mph).

● They can travel at tremendous speeds (clocked up to 16,000 mph) just as angels can do (Daniel 10:4, 12-13).

● Many UFO "contactees" have received "messages" of a telepathic or mediumistic nature such as the Bible connects with demons (1 Timothy 4:1f.).

● The content of UFO messages often carries things of religious significance that are contrary to the Bible (1 Timothy 4:1) (Alexander 1977, 1.2.14-19).

● Many new religions or cults have originated around messages from UFO beings.

● Some people have reported being "possessed" by UFO beings after contacts with them.

Taken as a whole, this evidence is a powerful indication that some UFO encounters of a "third kind" are demonically inspired.

7. *Evidence from demon possession*

Not everyone who thinks he is demon-possessed is really indwelt by a demon. Many of these people are hallucinating, and others are under the influence of drugs. But some cases cannot be totally explained in a purely normal way. Even Christian psychiatrists, trained in detecting purely psychological problems, acknowledge the reality of demon possession. Based on years of medical, biblical, and psychiatric training, Dr. Paul Meier emphatically confessed, "I personally believe in their existence" (Korem 1981, 153). Missionaries, evangelists, and Christian counselors have had wide experience with demon possession. (See Koch 1972.)

Going To and Fro in the Earth. The devil is active in the world. He is "roaming through the earth and going back and forth in it" (Job 1:6). He "prowls around like a roaring lion looking for someone to devour" (1 Peter 5:8). He does not appear in red pajamas with a pitchfork. Rather, he "masquerades as an angel of light" (2 Corinthians 11:14). According to the Bible, Satan and his demons are involved in the following activities:

1. *Demons provoke rebellion against God.*

Satan began in rebellion against God (1 Timothy 3:6; Revelation 12:4). Presently he is the "spirit who is now at work in those who are disobedient" (Ephesians 2:2). In the end of the age he will lead the great rebellion against God of which Paul wrote to the Thessalonians saying, "For that day will not come until the rebellion occurs and the man of lawlessness is revealed. . . . He will oppose and will exalt himself over everything that is called God" (2 Thessalonians 2:3-4).

2. *Demons inspire idolatry.*

Demons also instigate the worship of idols. Moses warned Israel not to "sacrifice their sacrifices to the goat demons" (Leviticus 17:7, NASB). He speaks of God's jealousy and anger because they "sacrificed to demons, which are not God" (Deuteronomy 32:17). Paul reminded the converted pagans

at Corinth that "the sacrifices of pagans are offered to demons, not to God. . . ." He adds, "I do not want you to be
participants with demons" (1 Corinthians 10:20).

3. *Demons instigate false teachings and religions.*

Not only are demons behind false gods but they also inspire false teachings. Paul exhorted Timothy to be aware that
"in later times some will abandon the faith and follow deceiving spirits and things taught by demons" (1 Timothy 4:1).
These include teachings that "forbid people to marry and
[that] order them to abstain from certain foods" (v. 3). The
apostle John is equally clear about the demonic influence
behind false teaching about Christ in the flesh: "Dear friends,
do not believe every spirit, but test the spirits to see whether
they are from God, because many false prophets have gone
out into the world" (1 John 4:1). Similar warnings are found
in other passages of Scripture (2 Timothy 3; 2 Peter 2; Jude 1;
Revelation 18).

4. *Demons seduce people to immorality.*

Immorality and idolatry go hand in hand. Both are practiced in pagan temples. Both are connected by Paul in Romans 1 where he speaks of men serving "created things
rather than the Creator" (v. 25). He adds, "Because of this,
God gave them over to shameful lusts" (v. 26). The same
connection is made in Ephesians 2 where the apostle speaks
of the "spirit who is now at work in those who are disobedient." This is one who encourages "gratifying the cravings of
our sinful nature" (vv. 2-3). According to Jude the "angels
that sinned" (i.e., demons) are the example followed by
"Sodom and Gomorrah . . .[who] gave themselves up to sexual immorality and perversion" (v. 7).

5. *Demons inflict injury and death.*

The devil delighted in inflicting disaster on Job (Job 1:12).
The writer of Hebrews informs us that the "one who holds
the power of death—that is, the devil" was defeated by
Christ (2:14). Indeed, the serpent (Satan) tried to kill Christ
(Genesis 3:15). John tells us that Satan "stood in front of the
woman who was about to give birth [to Christ], so that he
might devour her child the moment it was born" (Revelation
12:4). Demons delight in destruction and death. The demon

in the little boy caused him to "fall into the fire or into the water" (Matthew 17:15). The demonic desire to destroy by death makes them a sinister source of war. John speaks of demons who "go out to the kings of the whole world, to gather them for the battle on the great day of God Almighty [at Armageddon]" (Revelation 16:14).

6. *Demons inflict many sicknesses.*

Not all sickness is inflicted by demons. Some illnesses merely result from this being a fallen world (Genesis 3:14-19; Romans 8:18-25). The Bible clearly distinguishes between those who were "sick" and others who were influenced by the Devil (Matthew 8:16). However, there are many instances in which demons inflicted diseases such as muteness (Matthew 8:32), blindness (Matthew 12:22), deformity (Luke 13:1f.), seizures (Matthew 17:15f.), and others (Acts 10:38; 2 Corinthians 12:7). God desires to heal His creatures, but Satan desires to hurt them. God desires that they be well; the Devil wants them to be sick.

7. *Satan desires to deceive.*

The Devil is by nature a deceiver. He deceived Eve (Genesis 3:1f.; 1 Timothy 2:14). There are many aspects of his work in this regard. Satan "is the father of lies" (John 8:44). He tempts (1 Chronicles 21:1; Matthew 4:1f.). Satan also blinds (2 Corinthians 4:4) and ensnares (2 Timothy 2:26). He deceives in order to devour (1 Peter 5:8). He is the master liar and has two great lies:

"You will not surely die" (Genesis 3:4);

"You shall be like God" (Genesis 3:4).

While denying death he destroys the living. While he deifies man into God, he attempts to destroy man made in God's image.

8. *Demons oppress and "possess" people.*

Oppression is external influence of demons on individuals. The Book of Acts informs us that Jesus "went about doing good, and healing all who were oppressed by the devil" (Acts 10:38, NASB). But demons also "possess" some individuals, that is they exercise internal control over them. This "possession" is described several ways in the Bible. Some people are "demonized" (*daimonizomai*). The Canaanite woman cried out to Jesus: "My daughter is cruelly demon-possessed" (Matthew 15:22, NASB). Others are said to be "with" (en) an unclean spirit (Mark 1:23). Some are said to "have" (exonta) an evil spirit (Mark 9:17). And some demons are said to use a human body as their "house" (Matthew 12:44). Whatever the description, demon "possession" is a control exercised over individuals from the inside. There are many characteristics of those "possessed" by demons.

1. Severe sickness (Matthew 12:22).
2. Psychic powers (Acts 16:16).
3. Unusual physical strength (Mark 5:3).
4. Fits of rage (Mark 5:4).
5. Other personalities living within (Mark 5:6-7).
6. Different voices from within (Mark 5:9).
7. Resistant to spiritual help (Mark 5:7).
8. Hypersensitivity (Mark 5:7).
9. Involvement in occult practices (Deuteronomy 18:10-11).

Of course, no one of these is a necessary sign of demon possession. But these symptoms are like the warning signs of cancer. When they persist, one should consult a spiritual counselor trained to detect the demonic.

While demon influence is real, one cannot contract this spiritual "disease" by casual contact. Demons never enter uninvited. One must open the door for them by:

1. Yielding to sin (John 8:14).
2. Spiritual stubbornness or rebellion (1 Samuel 15:23).
3. Occult practices such as astrology, mediums (channelers), fortune-tellers, trying to contact the dead, etc. (Deuteronomy 18:11).
4. Transfer of occult powers (by some ritual).

These all involve free and deliberate acts. No one is "zapped" by demons against their will. People freely invite them into their lives by a combination of moral rebellion and occult association.

Distinguishing the Divine from the Demonic

A miracle has the "fingerprints" of God on it (see chapter 2). It is Godlike. A demonic sign is also like its source. Since

Satan is the "father of lies," it is not strange that the Bible speaks of his signs as "counterfeit miracles, signs and wonders" (2 Thessalonians 2:9).

Satanic "Signs." The Bible uses the same words to describe the powers of Satan as those used for miracles, namely, signs, wonders, and power (see Appendix 7). However, Satan's powers are not divine. In this sense his special works are "counterfeit miracles" (2 Thessalonians 2:9). God's power is infinite but Satan's power is limited. Indeed, the Devil has been officially defeated by the death and resurrection of Christ who "disarmed the powers and authorities . . .[and] made a public spectacle of them, triumphing over them by the cross" (Colossians 2:14). Hebrews declares that "by his death he . . . destroy[ed] him who holds the power of death— that is, the devil" (Hebrews 2:14). Despite his official defeat at the cross, Satan and his host are still at work in the world, awaiting their eternal sentence (Revelation 20). Meanwhile, they are exercising their powers to deceive. Satan's powers are not purely natural in the sense of mere physical forces, such as gravity or magnetism. But neither are they supernatural in the sense that God is supernatural. Rather, the Bible calls them "spiritual forces" (Ephesians 6:12) or "powers." Satan is the Master Mind of evil. Just as our human minds can and do affect the physical world, so Satan's finite but super mind can do so even more.

In spite of Satan's super power, he cannot do truly supernatural things as God can do. For example, he cannot create life or raise the dead. Although it is a debated point, Satan probably cannot suspend natural laws, but he can certainly utilize them in unusual ways for his own purposes. We know that he can cause a "fire . . . from the sky" and even cause "a mighty wind" (Job 1:12, 14, 19). Of course, modern science can do things like this, too. In this sense Satan is the Super Scientist. As such he can perform advanced wonders of science that seem to be supernatural but are not. Satan cannot create life, but he can clone it. In fact, he violates God's copyrights regularly. Satan does not need to be able to violate natural laws, as long as he can convince people he can do it.

Likewise, Satan is a Master Magician. He can perform

tricks that would baffle the greatest magicians. He is not able to do true miracles, but he certainly can fool people into thinking that he can. So for all practical purposes his powers seem miraculous. Indeed, John speaks of "the spirits of demons performing miraculous signs" (Revelation 16:14). Inspired by Satan, the Antichrist will display "all kinds of counterfeit miracles, signs and wonders" (2 Thessalonians 2:9). Jesus will even pronounce doom on some who claimed: "Lord, Lord, did we not prophesy in your name, and in your name drive out demons and perform many miracles?" (Matthew 7:22).

However, Satan's powers do not equal God's, as the contest between Moses and the magicians of Egypt reveals. They could emulate only some of the signs but begged off when God by Moses' hand created life from dust. They cried, "This is the finger of God" (Exodus 8:19).

"The Devil Made Me Do It"—But How? Part of the problem in identifying a work of demons as opposed to a purely magical or strictly normal event is the general misapprehension of the way in which the Devil works. These views often include one or more of the following mistakes:
1. Granting truly unlimited power to the Devil such as God alone possesses.
2. Assuming that the Devil works independently of the natural world rather than through it.
3. Separating the work of the Devil from the world and the flesh.
    This last error can be diagrammed as follows:

Wrong View

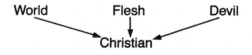

This diagram assumes that the Christian has three separate enemies: the world, the flesh, and the Devil. It believes that these three enemies work independently on the Christian. For example, it believes one can be worldly or fleshly without being affected by the Devil. We often speak of "worldly" Christians or "carnal" (fleshly) Christians whom we would not think of as "demonized" (i.e., influenced by the Devil).

But this is not the biblical view at all. The correct view is one in which the Devil works through the world system in which we live in the flesh in order to get at our soul. It can be diagrammed as follows:

Correct View

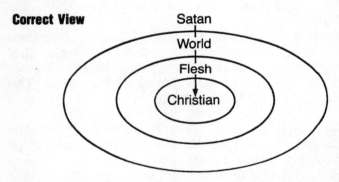

The Bible declares that "the whole world is under the control of the evil one" (1 John 5:19). Paul called the Devil "the ruler of the kingdom of the air" (Ephesians 2:2). Jesus referred to him as "the prince of this world." So the whole evil world system is energized by Satan and is opposed to God (2 Thessalonians 2:4).

The "world" system then is the evil sphere through which Satan works. Thus the Christian is told, "Do not love the world or anything in the world" (1 John 2:15). What is in the world? "Everything in the world [is]—the cravings of sinful man, the lust of the eyes and the boasting [pride] of what he has and does" (v. 16).

But these are the very areas of the "flesh" with which individual Christians struggle. For the "works of the flesh" include "sexual immorality, impurity, . . . selfish ambition, . . . and the like" (Galatians 5:19-21). So Satan working through the "world" system tempts Christians who participate in it through their "fleshly" (carnal) desires. The Devil wants to make us do it—but when we yield, it is because our own fleshly desires for the evil world system (of lust and pride) provide an opening by which he can influence our lives (see James 1:14). Those who do not live according to the flesh but according to the Spirit (Romans 8:4), are not vulnerable in this way.

The Devil never enters a life uninvited. He enters only disobedient hearts, for he is "the spirit who is now at work in those who are disobedient" (Ephesians 2:2). And the heavier influences of the Devil described as "possession" come only on individuals who live in stubborn disobedience. It is they who receive the unusual manifestations of occult powers. This is why the Scriptures say, "rebellion is like the sin of divination, and arrogance like the evil of idolatry" (1 Samuel 15:23). That is to say, the individual is made more vulnerable to occult and idolatrous influences through pride and disobedience. They are the "doors" of the flesh to the evil world that is energized by the Devil.

Earmarks of Satanic Signs. Satan is the Master Deceiver. He is the world's greatest counterfeiter. Many of his "signs" are, like those of earthly magicians, mere tricks. Others are advanced utilization of natural laws and mental powers. Whatever supernormal things he can do, none of them measure up the kind of supernatural things God can do. Only God can create life and raise the dead. Satan, however, is able to emulate much of what God does, at least enough to deceive many. Just as the magicians of Egypt were able to simulate some of the miracles God did through Moses, Satan imitates the supernatural today as well.

Much of what passes as "miracle" to the general public is simply magic or trickery (see chapter 5). Some are simply anomalies or unexplained natural occurrences (see chapter 4). Others, however, involve the intervention of evil spiritual powers. When demons are directly involved, one or more of the following characteristics will be present.

1. False predictions (Deuteronomy 18:21-22)
2. Contacting departed spirits (Deuteronomy 18:11)
3. Using instruments of divination, such as stones, cry-

stals, crystal balls (Deuteronomy 18:11a)
 4. Use of channelers, mediums, fortune-tellers or witches (Deuteronomy 18:11)
 5. Advocating idolatry or images (Exodus 20:3-4; Deuteronomy 13:1-3)
 6. Denial of deity or humanity of Christ (Colossians 2:9; 1 John 4:1-2)
 7. Advocating abstinence from certain foods for religious reasons (1 Timothy 4:3-4)
 8. Deprecating or denying marriage (1 Timothy 4:3)
 9. Promoting immorality (Ephesians 2:2-3; Jude 7)
10. Encouraging legalistic self-denial (Colossians 2:16-23)
11. Denying death (Genesis 3:4)
12. Encouraging self-deification (Genesis 3:5; 2 Thessalonians 2:9)
13. Promoting lying (John 8:44)
14. Advocating the practice of astrology (Deuteronomy 4:19; Isaiah 47:13-15).

Summary

When unusual events occur in connection with occult activities, the influence of demons is likely. When a person is a practitioner of special powers connected with these events, then demons have probably invaded that person's life. Without the presence of such practices, the activity is probably either magic (see chapter 5) or an anomaly (see chapter 4). On other occasions, demonic forces are more directly involved. They are even able to produce "signs and wonders." But these counterfeit miracles are not to be confused with true miracles (see chapters 2, 9). In short, the differences between divine miracles and demonic signs are as follows:

DIVINE MIRACLE	SATANIC SIGN
Supernatural	Supernormal
Connected with truth	Connected with error
Associated with good	Associated with evil
Never associated with occult	Often associated with occult
Always successful	Not always successful

8. Is There a Yardstick for Miracles?

Recognizing the Genuine and the Counterfeit

No one accepts Monopoly money for change in the grocery store. Why? Because it is not even a good imitation of real dollars. But many people have unwittingly accepted counterfeit money. The reason? Because a good counterfeit bill looks very much like the real thing. In this respect miracles are like money. The good counterfeits are like the genuine in appearance, at least to the untrained observer.

The Keys to Recognizing Counterfeits

There is another very important similarity between money and miracles. The counterfeit is distinguished from the genuine, not by the similarities, but the differences. No one would accept a Monopoly ten dollar bill for the real one on the grounds that both are rectangular, both are made of paper, and both have the same number on the face of them. Why? Because we do not determine what is counterfeit by its similarities to the genuine but by its differences from it. It is the differences that make the difference.

Only a trained observer can tell good counterfeit currency from the genuine. And the very good ones must be examined under a microscope to see those differences. Counterfeit miracles are the same. Only those skilled in the Scriptures can, under the microscope of God's Word, detect the most clever but bogus signs and wonders. Jesus said, "For false Christs and false prophets will appear and perform signs and miracles to deceive the elect—if that were possible" (Mark 13:22).

Just as the counterfeit must be measured over against the genuine, likewise error is known only in the light of the truth.

Unless we have a standard for what is right, we cannot hope to know what is wrong. For the Christian the Bible is the final measure of all error. Thus false miracles must be judged in the light of the true ones recorded in Scripture.

Interpreting Experiences by the Bible. All experiences, whether they are normal or supernormal, must be interpreted by the Bible rather than interpreting the Bible by our experiences. There is no doubt that hundreds of thousands of people have had experiences they believe to be supernatural. Contemporary advocates of signs and wonders often claim their experiences as a basis of their belief that New Testament miracles exist today. A case in point is John Wimber, who claims that "there is a sense in which our experience legitimately adds to the interpretation process." He adds, "I have talked with many evangelical theologians who have undergone significant changes in their theology because of an experience" (Wimber 1986, 88, 92). One example is a former professor at Dallas Seminary, Walter Bodine, who after being healed of emotional pain by John Wimber told *Christianity Today* that "any theological formulation that does not stand the test of Scripture and experience together needs to be reevaluated" (Frame 1988, 52).

We must be cautious with this kind of reasoning. Reevaluation of the Bible based on our experience often ends in reinterpreting the Bible by our experience, rather than interpreting our experience by the Bible. The Bible is our final authority, not our experience. Furthermore, experiences can be interpreted in different ways. For a Christian, all of life must be interpreted by the final authority of the Bible. Charismatic pastor Chuck Smith analyzed the problem well when he wrote:

One of the greatest weaknesses of the charismatic movement is its lack of sound Bible teaching. There seems to be an undue preoccupation with experience, which is often placed above the Word. As a consequence, charismatics have become a fertile field for strange and unscriptural doctrines proliferating through their ranks. (Smith 1983, 127)

There are many unusual experiences today. Some are of God and some are just odd (chapter 4). Some are supernatural and others are simply psychological (chapter 6). And some of these unusual experiences are divine and others are demonic (chapter 7). The Bible is the only infallible authority for determining which are which.

The Uniqueness of Biblical Miracles. Since we have already discussed the nature of a true miracle (chapter 2), we will summarize what we have learned. A biblical miracle is a truly supernatural act of God. As such, it has God's fingerprints on it. These include the following:

1. *A miracle is a supernatural act.* True miracles transcend natural law(s). They are a divine interference into the natural course of events. Real miraculous events are not simply unusual natural events. Rather, they are truly supernatural events. Miraculous healings in the Bible had the following characteristics (see chapter 2):

- They were always immediate.
- They were always successful, even on incurable diseases.
- They always lasted, with no relapses.
- They always glorified God by confirming His nature or His word (Hebrews 2:3-4).

2. *A miracle is always associated with truth.* True miracles are never associated with false teaching. There was a connection between the message and the miracle, between the sign and the sermon. Miracles provided divine confirmation of a new revelation. And the God of truth does not confirm error. So false teaching is never connected with true miracles.

3. *A miracle is always associated with good.* Since God is

morally good and miracles are His acts, it follows that miracles will manifest His moral character. It will bring glory to Him. If evil is manifest through a sign, then it is not a sign from God. John wrote, "This the first of his miraculous signs, Jesus performed in Cana of Galilee. He thus revealed his glory" (John 2:11).

4. *A miracle fits into nature.* Miracles are supernatural but not *anti*natural (see chapter 4). They are not square pegs in round holes; they fit. Sometimes they involve a speeding up of a natural process. But they are never against nature. What God does has purpose and design.

Characteristics of False Signs. In view of these unique characteristics of a genuine miracle we can now see by contrast what a counterfeit sign is. Since a counterfeit is known by its differences from the genuine, a false sign will differ from a true miracle in these ways:

1. *A false sign is not really supernatural.* False signs are unusual. They may even be supernormal, but they are not truly supernatural. They are extraordinary but not really miraculous. In this regard, they can be recognized as false signs if:

- They are not successful.
- They are not immediate or instantaneous.
- There is a relapse to the former condition.

2. *A false sign is associated with error.* False signs and false teaching go together. "The Spirit clearly says that in later times some will abandon the faith and follow deceiving spirits and things taught by demons" (1 Timothy 4:1). There is "a spirit of truth and a spirit of falsehood" (1 John 4:6). So false teaching will not be confirmed by a true miracle. Only false signs will be connected with false teachings. A true prophet does not give false prophecies. If the predicted sign does not come to pass, then it was a false sign. There are several false teachings connected with false signs, such as:

- Teaching that there are gods other than the one true God (Deuteronomy 6:4; 13:1-3)
- Teaching the use of images or idols in worship (Exodus 20:3-4)

- Teaching that Jesus is not God (Colossians 2:9)
- Teaching that Jesus did not come in human flesh (1 John 4:1-2)
- Teaching that we should contact departed spirits (Deuteronomy 18:11)
- Teachings (predictions) about the future that do not come to pass (Deuteronomy 18:21-22)
- Teaching prophecy without Christ at the center (Revelation 19:10)

3. *A false sign is associated with evil or occult practices.* Another characteristic of counterfeit miracles is evil or immorality. According to the Bible one or more of the following evil practices is associated with false signs.

- Moral rebellion and anger with God (1 Samuel 15:23)
- Sexual immorality (Jude 7)
- Denying the use of sex within marriage (1 Corinthians 7:5; 1 Timothy 4:3)
- Legalism and self denial (Colossians 2:16-23)
- Lying (1 Timothy 4:2; John 8:44)
- Abstaining from certain foods on spiritual grounds (1 Timothy 4:3-4)
- Contacting departed spirits (Deuteronomy 18:11)
- Use of channelers, mediums, or trances (Deuteronomy 18:11; 1 Corinthians 14:32)
- Use of crystals, stones, rods or other means of divination (Deuteronomy 18:11; Ezekiel 21:21)
- Encouraging self-deification (Genesis 3:5; 2 Thessalonians 2:9)
- Promoting astrology (Deuteronomy 4:19; Isaiah 47:13-15)
- Denying the deity or humanity of Christ (Colossians 2:9; 1 John 4:1-2)

4. *A false sign does not fit with nature.* False signs are unusual, but unlike miracles they are often odd. A true miracle fits with nature, but false signs are misfits. There is something unnatural about them. They do not fit the context. False signs are often forms of magic. Rabbits do not really come from hats, nor birds out of midair. This is all very odd. Likewise, false signs are often characterized by their oddness.

Putting Contemporary Signs and Wonders to the Test

Today's Christian is surrounded by a veritable supermarket of the supernormal. We are like a modern Alice in "signs and wonders" land (see chapter 1). This maze of the seemingly miraculous has called forth two extreme reactions, both of which should be avoided.

On the one hand are those, like the "Amazing Randi," who reject the miraculous altogether. They throw out the "baby" of miracles with the "bath water" of magic. They reject the truth of miracles because some have been caught doing the tricks of magic. But, as we have seen, there is no valid scientific or rational basis for rejecting *all* miracles (chapter 3). Just because many unusual events can be explained as magic (chapter 5) does not mean that all can. In fact, the false are made possible only because of the true. Counterfeits point to the existence of the genuine. Just because there is counterfeit currency in circulation does not mean we should stop believing in genuine dollars.

On the other extreme are naive and gullible people who have a tendency to believe most of what they read in the newspaper or see on TV. This seems especially true if the event is sensational, unusual, or incredible. It is unfortunately true that the general public is rather gullible and easily deceived. In spite of our modern pride in being educated and enlightened, the fact remains that many people, even the highly educated, are suggestible and gullible. Unhappily, this susceptibility is not limited to non-Christians.

What is needed is thoughtful openness to the reality of truth combined with helpful skepticism about the possibility of error. We must be willing to accept what is truly supernatural without being eager to believe everything unusual is supernatural. In order to make sense out of the current sensation of "signs and wonders" we need to think carefully and critically about what we are seeing. The Bible tells us: "Do not believe every spirit, but test the spirits to see whether they are from God, because many false prophets have gone out into the world" (1 John 4:1).

Even in the exercise of supernatural gifts in the New Testament there were checks and balances. Those who spoke in tongues needed someone to interpret (1 Corinthians 14:13).

Likewise, when one gave a prophecy, Paul declared that "others should pass judgment on what is said" (1 Corinthians 14:29, NASB). Let us apply this same kind of caution to the claims about signs and wonders today.

Testing Channelers and Mediumistic Messages. Actress Shirley MacLaine has made popular an alleged supernormal experience that has been common in occult religions for thousands of years. Her channeler, Kevin Ryerson, conveyed a message on national TV as millions of people watched. Was this a miracle? Was it of God? Using the above criteria, we can easily see that the answer to these questions is negative. Ryerson's experience violates several of the criteria of a true miracle.

First of all, it involves a medium. And God declared emphatically to Israel, "Let no one be found among you who . . . is a medium or spiritist or who consults the dead. Anyone who does these things is detestable to the LORD" (Deuteronomy 18:10-12).

Second, true miracles from God do not come in a trance or altered state of consciousness. These are means used by mediums and channelers but not by the Holy Spirit. Former pagans in the church at Corinth had experienced this kind of overpowering by spirits, but Paul made it very clear to them that "the spirits of prophets are subject to the control of prophets" (1 Corinthians 14:32). That is to say, whatever comes from God is under the prophet's control. God never violates the will of His servants in revealing Himself to them.

When someone is overpowered by a force beyond his control, it is not of God. God spoke to people in visions (1 Corinthians 12) and through dreams while in a natural state of sleep (Genesis 15; Daniel 7). But God never zapped anyone into a state of unconsciousness and then revealed Himself to them. Serving God involves having freedom and dignity. God never violates His image in humans in order to reveal Himself to them.

Finally, there is false teaching and a false God of pantheism connected with the "revelations" involved in Shirley MacLaine's channeler. In her popular book *Dancing in the Light* she urges her followers to claim they are God by chanting, "I am God or I am that I am as Christ often did, or you can extend the affirmations to fit your own needs." This, of course, is blasphemy for a Christian and is a sure indication that the source of this lie is the "father of lies" who first seduced Adam and Eve to believe "You will be like God" (Genesis 3:5).

Testing "Slaying in the Spirit." John Wimber, an important figure in the "signs and wonders" movement, describes the phenomenon known as "slaying in the spirit" as follows:

People fell to the floor. Others, who did not believe in tongues, loudly spoke in tongues. The speaker roamed among the crowd, praying for people, who then immediately fell over with the Holy Spirit resting on them. (Wimber 1986, 24)

Wimber asked for a sign from God that this was something He—not humans or Satan—was doing. A phone call from a fellow pastor who had the same experience convinced Wimber.

A few years ago my former travel agent asked me what I thought of being "slain in the Spirit." Not knowing her well, I was hesitant to offer my frank opinion. She seemed urgent to know and pressed me for an answer. I delayed by asking her why she was asking about it. She said that she and her husband and most of the leaders in the same church they had recently attended were all "slain in the Spirit." But within months of this experience all of those involved were either divorced or suing for divorce. Her husband had just announced his intentions to divorce her. Then I told her what I thought.

First, being "slain in the Spirit" is not of God because, like a trance, it puts one in an altered state of consciousness. As we have just discussed, God does not work this way. These kinds of states can be produced either hypnotically or demonically.

Second, notice that Wimber's justification was not Scripture but experience. Though he does appeal to Scripture, he sometimes seems to misinterpret it. For example, he compares people who were conscious while God worked in their lives (Ezekiel, Paul, John) to someone who is unconscious as he is being "slain in the spirit." Further, he compares the conscious state of fear the soldiers at the tomb had when they saw an angel with the unconscious state after being "slain in the spirit." This is a classic example of reading one's experience into the Bible. It violates the principle that the experience should be judged by the Bible and not the Bible by the experience.

Third, if the experience is connected with evil then it cannot be of God. Obviously, this was the case related by my travel agent. The Bible is clear: "'I hate divorce,' says the Lord" (Malachi 2:16). Jesus said, "Anyone who divorces his wife and marries another woman commits adultery" (Mark 10:10). So whatever it was that overpowered them and led to their divorces apparently was not of God.

Testing Raising the Dead. From time to time there are reports that people are being raised from the dead. If so, then this would be a true miracle. Jesus raised the dead (John 11) and so did His apostles (Matthew 10:8; Acts 9:40; 20:9-10). John Wimber says that one of the healing ministries we are called to perform today is the "healing of the dying and the dead. This involves both comforting and strengthening those who are dying, and—infrequently—raising the dead" (Wimber 1987, 62). However, there are good reasons to believe that no human beings have the power to do that today.

First of all, the power to raise the dead was a special "sign of an apostle" (2 Corinthians 12:12), and there are no apostles today. Jesus chose twelve apostles "and gave them authority" to "raise the dead" (Matthew 10:1, 8). This special power was used on several occasions. Paul raised both Dorcas (Acts 9) and Eutychus (Acts 20) from the dead. There is no record in the New Testament that Jesus gave this power to anyone other than apostles.

Not only is the ability to raise the dead a unique power that God only granted to apostles in the New Testament, but apostles lived only in the time of the New Testament. For the condition of being an apostle stated by the apostles is that one "must become a witness with us of his resurrection"

(Acts 1:22). Paul reiterated this when he declared to the Corinthians, "Am I not an apostle? Have I not seen Jesus our Lord?" (1 Corinthians 9:1). But it is obvious that to have seen the resurrected Christ then one would have had to live during the time of Christ. So no one since the first century could possibly be an apostle.

The "signs of an apostle" passed away with the times of an apostle. How then do we explain the many claims that these New Testament signs and wonders, including raisings from the dead, still exist today? The claims for resurrection fall into several categories.

First, some alleged raisings from the dead are simply fraudulent tricks. A witch doctor announced to some startled villagers that the gods were cursing the village. Someone must die, he said. Dramatically he grabbed a gun, called the offender forward, and shot him. The blood spurted from the man's chest and he fell dead. He was placed in a box and buried. Three days later the witch doctor proclaimed the gods were satisfied and the man would rise from the dead. The people gathered and watched young men dig down to the box, open it, and see the man sit up in the coffin and be helped to his feet (Kole 1984, 11-12). When the well-known magician Andre Kole examined this alleged resuscitation, which took place in Liberia, he uncovered a clever plot in which the witch doctor prearranged with the victim to place a balloon full of pig blood under his shirt. When the witch doctor fired a blank shot the man grasped his chest, puncturing the balloon from which the blood gushed out. After that he was placed in the coffin and escaped through a trapdoor and hid for three days. He returned and emerged from the grave on cue from the witch doctor.

Second, some alleged raisings from the dead involve mystically induced "comas." Some Indian gurus are able to slow down their bodily processes by altering their state of consciousness. This enables them to spend hours in a grave with little oxygen. In October 1987 there was a network TV special celebrating the sixty-first anniversary celebration of Houdini's death. On it one magician was buried alive under nine feet of dirt. He emerged alive from his coffin an hour and a half later. But he made no claim to death and resurrection. He was simply a great escape artist who somehow managed to utilize the oxygen from his large coffin while digging his way to the surface.

Third, some cases are simply medical resuscitations, not actually resurrections. Medical science performs resuscitations regularly on people who are clinically but not actually dead. This can be done by some sort of shock to the heart or air to the lungs. But in neither case is it actually bringing back the soul of someone who was physically dead. When Jesus raised Lazarus from the dead, he had been buried for four days, and his body was already decomposing (John 11:39).

Fourth, some alleged raisings are merely cases where the individuals fainted or went into a coma. Early in 1987 well-known TV evangelist Oral Roberts claimed to have raised many people from the dead. However, when asked for names and addresses of them, he declined. Later, he mentioned one girl who had passed out in his service. When asked how he knew she was dead, he cited the fact that her body felt cold and that both he and the girl's mother believed she was dead. This kind of "evidence" hardly convinces a committed believer, let alone a skeptic.

The resurrections claimed in the Indonesian revivals (Tari 1971) were also probably not real deaths. When professor George Peters researched the matter firsthand, he found no evidence of real physical resurrections. He discovered, rather, that the word for death in their culture included states of unconsciousness, such as fainting and comas (see Peters 1973, ch. 5).

Claims of resurrections are still made today, but the evidence is very strong that these are not real physical resurrections from the dead. If anyone had this kind of power, they would be thronged by crowds and newspaper reporters. Jesus had to continually pledge people to silence about His miracles (Matthew 8:4; 17:9). Even then He was so thronged with crowds that He often did not have time to eat (Mark 6:31; John 6:24). Any living person with these kinds of powers would be headlined around the world. The truth is that no one since the time of the apostles is known to have possessed these kinds of powers.

The ability to raise the dead was a special sign of an apostle, and there have been no apostles since the first century (Acts 1:22). This does not mean that God cannot raise the dead. He most assuredly can and will raise the dead—all of them at the end of the age (John 5:28-30; Revelation 20:4-5). It simply means that there is no evidence that anyone today possesses this special apostolic gift of being able to raise the dead.

Testing Healings. The "signs and wonders" movement claims that hundreds, even thousands, of people are being healed around the world. John Wimber claims that "today we see hundreds of people healed every month in Vineyard Christian Fellowship services" (Wimber 1986, 55). He tells of a woman who "was healed of about 80 percent of her condition" and others who "slowly" recovered of their illnesses (Wimber 1986, 96, 100, 104). But when Jesus or the apostles healed people they were 100 percent cured—immediately.

Wimber describes how he became aware of his power of healing. He got it while he was unconscious. Later, when he awoke from his sleep, his wife, Carol, told him that she had laid his hand on her and she was healed. His hand was still hot from the power that passed through it (Wimber 1987, 32). According to Wimber, Carol "reasoned that if God had filled her with the Holy Spirit while sleeping, he could work the same way in me." (Wimber does state at this point that this healing incident did not immediately convince him that he should practice divine healing.)

Oral Roberts acknowledged that he sometimes asked viewers seeking healing to place a glass of water on the television and then drink it after he had prayed for their healing. He also shared that he had been healed by an old Indian. Occult expert Kurt Koch concluded that Roberts "originally received these mediumistic powers from the old Indian who once healed him in his younger days" (Koch 1976, 54). Whatever the source of contemporary healers' powers, the evidence clearly indicates that they are definitely not the New Testament gift of healing. This is evident for several reasons.

First, the use of physical objects as a means of healing is

more in line with occult means of divination condemned in the Bible (Deuteronomy 18:11). The same is true of becoming aware of healing powers by physical contact with someone else, such as John Wimber apparently did with his wife. This power does not differ in kind from those in other religions. And, as we have seen, these kinds of powers are an indication of a false sign, not a true miracle.

Second, biblical miracles were neither gradual nor partial, as Wimber confessed that many of his were. God never performed a miracle "slowly" nor did an "80 percent " healing. Biblical miracles were 100 percent and immediate. In the case of the few immediate cures in the contemporary signs and wonders movement, most are clearly of the psychosomatic type and none are immediate healings of incurable diseases (see chapter 6). There is nothing supernatural about these kinds of cures.

Such cures are done regularly by Hindu gurus and by many other false religions and cults. Even non-Christian doctors and counselors witness these kinds of cures in their patients. Both spontaneous remission and psychosomatic cures of the same nature as these "signs and wonders" occur apart from any pretense to the supernatural.

Fourth, Wimber shows other indications that his power of healing is psychic in origin, not a supernatural gift from God. There are two evidences of this in his own writings. First of all, he received his power while he was in rebellion against God. He recalls that over a ten-month period, "I became angry with God many times" (Wimber 1987, 14). The anger was because God was not using him to bring about healings.

The Bible makes it clear that one does not receive what Wimber calls "filling with the Spirit" when they are angry with God. In fact, we are told in Scripture that even overnight anger is the way to "give the devil a foothold" (Ephesians 4:27). And to be filled with the Holy Spirit one needs to yield to God (Ephesians 5:18). Certainly a state of continued anger with God is not one in which He conveys divine powers. As Samuel exhorted Saul, "rebellion is like the sin of divination" (1 Samuel 15:23). There is a close connection between rebellion and witchcraft; rejecting God's authority in one's life opens him up to accepting another's authority.

The next indication of the psychic origin of Wimber's power to heal was that he received it suddenly—literally overnight. In spite of the fact that he had tried many times to heal people with continual failure, he suddenly received the power to perform these kinds of healings by the hands of his wife. This is more of a sign of psychic power, not a divine gift.

Another evidence that Wimber's powers are not of divine origin is that fact that he received them in a state of unconsciousness (Wimber 1987, 32). God's power to heal is not revealed to people in unconscious states. Even in the miracle that Christ did not appear to initiate, He was nonetheless consciously aware that the power of God had flowed through Him. For when the woman touched the hem of His garment, "at once Jesus realized that power had gone out from him" (Mark 5:30). Paul informed the Corinthians that God's power never overwhelms His prophets. For "the spirits of prophets are subject to the control of prophets" (1 Corinthians 14:32). The supernatural power of God does not zap people into unconsciousness. (See Edgar 1983, 81, 149, 245.)

Even those to whom God spoke while they were not aware that He was speaking to them were nevertheless not unconscious while He was speaking to them. For God spoke to them while they were consciously dreaming (Daniel 7; Matthew 1) or having a vision (Daniel 2; 2 Corinthians 12). But God never "slays" anyone in the Spirit or knocks them unconscious or manifests His supernatural gifts through them while they are not conscious. The prophets were not always fully aware of the implications of everything God was saying or doing through them (see 1 Peter 1:10-12). But even though they were not always aware that their gift was in operation, nevertheless, they were always conscious when their gifts were being exercised. For, as Paul said, the prophets' gifts were under the prophets' control. But Wimber exercised his power to heal his wife when he was not in control but was unconscious.

This is not to say that Wimber, Oral Roberts, and other healers are not believers. It is simply to say that even believers are not immune to deception. Even a sincere believer can be wrong. Hence, the apostle urges believers to "test the spirits to see whether they are from God" (1 John 4:1).

Testing Special "Revelations from God." God cannot err (Hebrews 6:18), but many of the "revelations" being received today are mistaken. Therefore, they cannot be of God. To speak of fallible revelations from God is a contradiction in terms (see Appendix 3). There are numerous examples of false "revelations" both inside and outside Christian circles. Joseph Smith, the founder of Mormonism, is a case in point. Mormons believe he was a prophet of God. Yet Joseph recorded numerous "revelations" that are known to be false. For example, Smith predicted on August 2, 1833, that "Zion [Missouri] cannot fall or be moved out of her place" (Smith 1974, Sect. 97). But unknown to Smith, who was in Kirtland, Ohio, two weeks earlier (July 20, 1833) Zion was moved, their printing presses were destroyed, and the Mormon officials were run out of town.

Untrue revelations are not unique to religious cults. Unfortunately, many Christians are claiming to receive revelations from God. But their results are not noticeably better than unbelievers. For example, David Wilkerson predicted that within a "few" years after 1973 an earthquake would wipe out one-third of the United States (Wilkerson 1974, 35). It did not happen. Pat Robertson of "The 700 Club" predicted in 1969 that the stock market was about to crash (Robertson 1984, 193). This did not happen either. Other Christian leaders inspire their followers by claiming that "God said" this or that to them.

One well-known international Christian leader told his thousands of followers that God told him to buy several thousand acres and build a university. He bought it, but it turned out to be a financial fiasco. The property was not approved for building the university. Was God wrong? Or is it not more likely that God had not really said this, but that the man was simply sharing his own well-intended desire? One lady told me that God told her to divorce her husband. God, however, has already declared Himself very clearly to the contrary (Malachi 2:14; Mark 10:10).

Those who claim to receive these "revelations" usually give a false test for their authenticity. Most often it is a subjective test, such as feeling. Jessica Hahn, of Jim Bakker and PTL fame, is reported to have asked God for a sign as to whether she should pose for *Playboy* magazine. While posing, she reportedly looked up and saw a rainbow in the sky (no doubt with a pot of gold at the end of it!). She took the rainbow as a sign of God's approval on her activity. Here again, subjective experience is used to go contrary to the Word of God which declares clearly what a rainbow means (Genesis 9:12-16).

Pastor Chuck Smith recognized this problem of interpreting the Bible by our experience when he wrote:

Any time we begin to allow our experiences to become the criteria for doctrine or belief, we have lost biblical authority, and the inevitable result is confusion. There are so many people who witness of remarkable and exciting experiences. The Mormons, for example, "bear witness" to the truth of the Book of Mormon. . . . One person says he has experienced that it is true, and another says he has experienced that it is false. Which one am I to believe? Each one swears he has had a true experience from God; yet one has to be wrong. Whenever you open the door for experience to become the foundation for doctrinal truth, you are opening Pandora's box. The result is that the truth is lost in the conflicting experiences, and the inevitable consequence is total confusion. We know that God is not the author of confusion. (Smith 1983, 127-128)

Conclusion

There are many "signs and wonders" occurring today. The vast majority of them give no evidence that they fit into the category of a New Testament miracle. Many of them are purely psychosomatic healings. On closer examination, some of them are bogus. The differences between a true miracle and a false sign can be summarized as follows:

TRUE MIRACLES	COUNTERFEIT MIRACLES
Actual supernatural acts	Extraordinary natural acts
Supernaturally directed	Naturally directed
Supernatural intervention	Natural operation
Always associated with truth	Always associated with error
Connected with true prophets	Connected with false prophets
Connected with biblical teaching	Connected with unbiblical teaching
Always associated with good	Always associated with evil
Glorify the Creator	Glorify the creature
Promote moral good which benefits God's creation	Promote moral evil which destroys God's creation
Fit with nature	Misfit with nature
Are not unnatural	Are unnatural (odd)

True miracles were performed by Jesus and the New Testament apostles. God gave them supernatural gifts in order to found the Christian church (Ephesians 2:20). It is evident that these special miraculous "signs of an apostle" are not in the possession of any individuals today. The signs of an apostle passed away with the times of an apostle (Hebrews 2:3-4).

Does this mean that there are no miracles today? Does it mean that God no longer heals in answer to the prayer? Is God no longer in the miracle-working business? As we shall see in the next chapter, the answer to these questions is a resounding no.

9. Do Miracles Occur Today?

"Miracles and healings of all kinds and classes should be received gladly. . . . They should be expected as part of the normal Christian life." So claims Richard Foster in his introduction to John Wimber's *Power Evangelism*. Wimber himself claims that all kinds of miraculous healings are occurring, even resurrection from the dead (Wimber 1987, 38, 62).

Professor C. Peter Wagner of Fuller Theological Seminary claims that "the great future breakthrough to the Buddhists, Hindus, and Muslims will be accompanied with signs and wonders in the New Testament style" (*Signs and Wonders Today*, 1983, 44). But are the New Testament sign gifts being manifested today? Do we possess the same powers to perform the signs and wonders done by the apostles in the early church? Has divine intervention ceased entirely?

Debunking the Skeptics

Some skeptics doubt whether miracles have ever occurred. They believe that a scientific attitude toward the world completely rules out the miraculous. But as we have already seen, the scientific evidence points to the creation of the world (see chapter 3). And if the world was created, then the big miracle has already occurred. If God has made the universe from nothing, then other supernatural acts are minor by comparison. Making water out of nothing is far more miraculous than making wine out of water. Once the first verse of the Bible is admitted, then the miracles of the rest of the Bible are all credible. "In the beginning God created the heavens and the earth." That is the big one. Everything else is small by comparison.

C. S. Lewis, the former atheist, put it succinctly: "If we admit God, must we admit Miracles? Indeed, you have no security against it. That is the bargain" (Lewis 1947, 109). For once we admit there is a God who can act supernaturally, then it follows that there can be supernatural acts of God. Total skepticism is unjustified. As long as there is a supernatural being (God), then He can act supernaturally. Total skepticism about miracles demands total atheism. As long as it is possible that God exists, then miracles are possible.

Thomas Jefferson spoke of both "Creator" and "creation" in the Declaration of Independence, but he denied the virgin birth and the resurrection of Christ. In fact, he literally cut all the miracles out of the four Gospels and pasted the rest together in a book. It was later published as *The Jefferson Bible*. It ends abruptly with these words: "There laid they Jesus, and rolled a great stone to the door of the sepulchre, and departed." But Jefferson was inconsistent. He admitted the big miraculous event of creating something from nothing but had difficulty with the lesser miraculous events of the virgin birth and resurrection of Christ. If God can accomplish the miraculous creation of the universe, then He can also accomplish the miracle of the Resurrection.

Supernatural Conversions

God can do miracles, and He has done them in the past. The Bible is replete with stories of miracles that God performed. God has done miracles from the parting of the Red Sea through Moses to the calling down of fire from heaven by Elijah to the resurrection of Lazarus by Jesus. Jesus healed the sick, opened the eyes of the blind, and raised the dead. Miracles not only can happen, but they have happened in significantly large numbers.

But do supernatural things still happen today? God used to do them, but does He still perform them? The answer is an emphatic yes. God is performing thousands of the most miraculous events since the creation of the world. Day by day hundreds and thousands of persons are undergoing the miraculous experience of the new creation. As Paul reminded the Corinthians, "If anyone is in Christ, he is a new creation; the old has gone, the new has come!" (2 Corinthians 5:17). This is the supernatural birth of which Jesus spoke when He said, "You must be born again" (John 3:7). By this miraculous transformation, sinners are declared saints, the wicked are made righteous in Christ. We are transformed from "darkness into his wonderful light" (1 Peter 2:9).

Creation is the greatest supernatural event of all, and the Bible makes a direct comparison of salvation to that of creation. Paul wrote that "God, who said.'Let light shine out of darkness,' made his light shine in our hearts" (2 Corinthians 4:6). Bringing spiritual light into the life of a child of darkness is a miraculous event comparable to that of the original creation of physical light. When we contemplate the untold thousands and even millions of people living today who have experienced this miraculous metamorphosis, how can we deny supernatural events in today's world?

Miraculous conversions occur by the thousands today all over the world. While many today are seeking signs, they are missing the greatest wonder of all. When the disciples returned rejoicing from their miracle-working tour, Jesus said, "Do not rejoice that the spirits submit to you, but rejoice that your names are written in heaven" (Luke 10:20).

All of us who have personally experienced this supernatural event know what a marvelous work of God's grace it is. The miraculous does happen today—every day—as God saves sinners. This is the greatest kind of supernatural event since the creation of the world, and it is happening thousands of times all over the world. These are the truly great wonders of our day.

Furthermore, it is a mistake to suppose that God only works in unusual ways when He saved someone from sickness as opposed to graciously helping them through it. Although many in the signs and wonders movement acknowledge that regeneration is a great miracle, we must agree with J. I. Packer, who stated,

There are many of us for whom the role model is Joni Eareckson rather than John Wimber. We see the power of the kingdom operating, but mainly in regeneration, sanctification, the Spirit as a comforter, the transformation of the inner life, rather than in physical miracles which just by happening prevent much of that other kingdom activity whereby people learn to live with their difficulties and glorify God. (Quoted in Stafford 1986)

In addition to God's miraculous work of *saving* grace, there is God's miraculous work of *sustaining* grace. God should not only be praised when He saves us from sickness but also when He sustains us through it. He said to Paul who prayed to be relieved of his thorn in the flesh, "My grace is sufficient for you" (2 Corinthians 12:9).

Does God Heal Today?

All Bible-believing Christians acknowledge that miraculous new births are occurring today, though some forget their importance. But does God still heal the sick today? Or were healings limited to Bible times? The answer to this is that God still answers prayer and still heals the sick in many ways.

First, God heals through the amazing bodily processes He has created. Doctors are the first to admit that they do not heal. The physician can set a bone, but only the Great Physician can cause it to grow together again.

Second, God also heals by inspiring good attitudes in us (see chapter 6). Faith is often an essential ingredient in recovery. We need to trust God for our physical as well as our spiritual well being.

Third, God heals through providing good food to eat. The Bible commends some foods (Proverbs 24:13) and beverages for health purposes (1 Timothy 5:23).

Fourth, God providentially intervenes in answer to prayer. I have personally experienced God's gracious hand of healing. Just after I was married to my wife, Barbara, I came down with a serious case of hepatitis. My liver stopped its normal functions. I was so weak that I could not even lift an arm. While lying in the hospital, the radio announced that the late Senator McCarthy died of hepatitis. My wife and the small congregation we served invoked God on my behalf. God heard their prayers and graciously restored me to health. Not only did I gradually regain all my strength, but I have suffered no ill effects for the past thirty years. I praise God for His goodness in healing me.

The Bible is clear as to what we should do when we are sick:

Is any one of you sick? He should call the elders of the church to pray over him and anoint him with oil in the name of the Lord. And the prayer offered in faith will make the sick person well; the Lord will raise him up. If he has sinned, he will be forgiven. Therefore confess your sins to each other and pray for each other so that you may be healed. (James 5:14-16)

I see no reason why this should not be taken literally. Many churches exercise this biblical practice with great profit to their members. God is concerned for all our needs, physical needs included. Indeed, Christ died for all our sickness and our sins (Isaiah 53:4-5; Matthew 8:16-17). However, the fact that our ultimate healing is in the atonement (Revelation 21:4) is no more a guarantee that we can claim healing for every sickness now than it is that we can avoid old age and death (Romans 5:12; 8:20-23). Our resurrection is in the atonement too, but we cannot claim it today. In fact, the ultimate "healing" of the body will not come until the resurrection, when we will receive the "redemption of our bodies" (Romans 8:23). Meanwhile, God graciously heals from time to time in accordance with His will and in response to "the prayer offered in faith" (James 5:15).

God normally heals through natural processes and good mental attitudes. Sometimes He brings about an unusual recovery in response to prayer. But does God still perform instantaneous cures of organic diseases? Or are all healings today psychosomatic-type cures of functional diseases? In short, does God ever perform supernatural healings today? Consider the case of Barbara Cummiskey.

A Case Study. At age fourteen Barbara was perfectly healthy. A year later her hand began to slip as she gripped the gymnastic rings. Doctors were sure she had multiple sclerosis (MS). In the next several years Barbara was ravaged by this crippling disease. Her bodily organs began to malfunction. A catheter was placed in her bladder. Breathing was so difficult that a tracheotomy was performed—cutting a hole in her neck so a respirator could be attached. Her vision worsened to the point of legal blindness. Several surgeries followed, as did three cardiac arrests. Lack of oxygen to her brain resulted in mental confusion.

Through her long ordeal, Barbara turned to God. She prayed simply but repeatedly in childlike prayers. Hearing of her plight, a local Christian radio station urged prayer on her behalf. Nearly 450 cards and letters flooded in to her. On June 7, 1981, two friends were reading cards to her. Barbara heard a voice over her shoulder (not the voices of her friends) saying, "My child, get up and walk." She had not walked in two years. Her legs were atrophied. Nevertheless, in simple faith she "jumped" out of bed and started down the hall where she met her mother who shouted "Calves! You have calves!" When Barbara met her father downstairs, they danced around the room. Barbara did ballet steps, standing on her toes and leaping.

Barbara's friend, an occupational therapist, told her, "You know, you just wrecked everything I learned in school." Barbara is still rejoicing in God's miraculous healing of her body (Clapp 1983, 16-17). Yes, God does heal today, sometimes in spectacular ways. Barbara Cummiskey is living testimony to the fact.

God does hear and answer our prayers, including prayers for healing. But He does not always need to perform a miracle to do so. God's wonderful works in our lives are accomplished through His special providence as well. Here is the difference between them.

PROVIDENCE	**MIRACLES**
Using natural law	Beyond natural law
By prearranging (indirectly)	By intervening (directly)
Gradually	Immediately
Can be duplicated by nature	Cannot be duplicated by nature

Although miracles are always possible, they are seldom necessary. For God can provide unusual answers to prayer by specially prearranging circumstances in an incredible way. God can so order the logistics of life as to bring about statistical improbabilities that, given the special spiritual circumstance, we can properly claim as the hand of God.

Do Miraculous Gifts Exist Today?

God can miraculously intervene in the world. He has done it in the past, and He is doing it in the present. Healings exist as a *fact*, but does the New Testament *gift* of healing exist today? Does anyone possess the same miraculous powers that the apostles had? To answer this question, let's take a look at who apostles were and what their special powers enabled them to do.

The Unique Ministry of Apostles. Not every follower of Christ was an apostle. Jesus had many followers, but He chose only twelve to be apostles (Matthew 10:1). To be an apostle, one had to be an eyewitness of the resurrected Christ. The stated qualification for the vacated office was that one "must become a witness . . . for his resurrection" (Acts 1:22). Paul met this qualification (1 Corinthians 15:7) and defended his apostleship to the Corinthians, saying, "Am I not an apostle? Have I not seen Jesus our Lord?" (1 Corinthians 9:1). So while there were more apostles than the original twelve (see Acts 14:14), the number was definitely limited. Paul said emphatically: "Not all are apostles" (1 Corinthians 12:29, NASB).

Apostles had a special task. They were the foundation of the Christian church. Jesus promised to guide them to "all truth" and bring to their remembrance "everything" He had taught them (John 14:26; 16:13). Paul declared that the church is "built on the foundation of the apostles and prophets, with Christ himself as the chief cornerstone" (Ephesians 2:20). Indeed, the early church "devoted themselves to the apostles' teaching" (Acts 2:42). Their special divine authority was exercised in both doctrine (Acts 15) and in discipline (Acts 5).

The apostles, like the Old Testament prophets, received divinely infallible revelation. Their revelations are written in the New Testament (1 Corinthians 2:10-13). These revelations were considered to be "Scripture" right alongside of the Old Testament (2 Peter 3:15-16). Their books were read in the churches (1 Thessalonians 5:27), passed on to other churches (Colossians 4:16), and collected by other believers (2 Peter 3:15-16). Indeed, their special miraculous powers were used to confirm that their teaching was from God. The miracles were a confirmation of their message (Hebrews 2:3-4).

The Unique Supernatural Powers of an Apostle. Not only did God give apostles the special task of founding the Christian church, but He also gave them special "sign" gifts to administer their task of founding and teaching the Christian church. From the very beginning the early church "devoted themselves to the apostles' teaching and . . . everyone was filled with awe, and many wonders and miraculous signs were done by the apostles" (Acts 2:42-43).

Later, the apostle Paul reminded the Corinthians that "the things that mark an apostle—signs, wonders and miracles—were done among you with great perseverance" (2 Corinthians 12:12). Since being an apostle was a special God-ordained task, it necessitated special divinely bestowed gifts.

1. *The apostolic gift of tongues*

Only the apostles received the gift of tongues at Pentecost (see Appendix 7). Others later received the same gift through "the laying on of the apostles hands" (Acts 8:18). Philip preached to the Samaritans and even did "great signs and miracles" (Acts 8:13) by the gifts that he received from the laying on of the apostles' hands (Acts 6:6; 2 Timothy 1:6). But even though God greatly blessed Philip's evangelistic efforts

in Samaria, the Samaritan believers did not receive the Holy
Spirit through his ministry. Only later when the apostles
came and laid hands on them did they receive the gift of the
Holy Spirit (8:15-18). The same was true for Cornelius and
the Italians (Acts 10:44-46) and for the Asians (Acts 19:1-6).
They were believers but did not receive the Holy Spirit or
speak in tongues except through an apostle.

Paul's personal wish that all could speak in tongues (1 Corinthians 14:5) was as unfulfillable as his desire that he could
be lost if Israel could be saved (Romans 9:3). And his exhor-
tation to "desire spiritual gifts" including tongues was given
to the whole church (the plural is used), not to each individual. For he clearly stated that only some were given tongues
(12:10, 30), and so only these were to seek to exercise them in
an orderly way (14:27). Further, the gift of tongues was a real,
knowable language (Acts 2:8), not an unintelligible utterance. The fact that the apostles spoke immediately and flu-
ently in a real language they had never learned marked this
as miraculous. The gift of tongues was a sign to unbelievers
(1 Corinthians 14:11). It was a special power that God provided the early church only to and through an apostle.

2. *Other special apostolic gifts*

Other supernatural gifts were also given by the laying on of
the apostles' hands. Paul, who had not seen the Christians at
Rome, said, "I long to see you so that I may impart to you
some spiritual gift to make you strong" (Romans 1:11). Paul
told Timothy: "Do not neglect your gift, which was given you
. . . when the body of elders laid their hands on you" (1 Timothy 4:14). That the elders here were apostles is made clear
when Paul later reminded Timothy "to fan into flame the
gift of God, which is in you through the laying on of my
hands" (2 Timothy 1:6). Apostles are called elders elsewhere
(2 John 1). They were elders by *office* (1 Timothy 3:1) but
apostles by *gift* (1 Corinthians 12:29; Ephesians 4:11). The
unique function of an apostle was that only they received
these special gifts and only they were able to give them to
others.

The Special Period of Sign Gifts. The apostles were a special
group of Christ's disciples with special gifts, and they lived

at a special time. According to Acts 1:22 an apostle had to be an eyewitness of the resurrected Christ. Paul explicitly states this as his qualification to be an apostle (1 Corinthians 9:1; 15:7). The author of Hebrews describes apostles as "those who heard him [Christ]" (Hebrews 2:3) and adds, "God also testified to it by signs, wonders and various miracles, and gifts of the Holy Spirit distributed according to his will" (v. 4).

It is also clear that apostles lived only in the first century. The twelve apostles were said to have been "eyewitnesses" of Jesus' earthly ministry (Luke 1:2), men present on earth when "Jesus went in and out among" them (Acts 1:21). As Jesus said to them, "You also must testify, for you have been with me from the beginning" (John 15:27). When Jesus later appeared to Paul, it was made clear that this was the "last of all" His appearances (1 Corinthians 15:8). Indeed, Hebrews 2:3 refers to the miraculous confirmation through the apostles as a past event "was confirmed." Writing after the time of miraculous apostolic confirmation in the Book of Acts, Jude speaks of the "faith that was once for all entrusted [in the past] to the saints" through the apostles (vv. 3, 17).

Contrasting Earlier and Later Use of Sign Gifts

There is a marked contrast in the use of sign gifts between earlier and later periods in the New Testament. This can be expressed in the following comparison.

EARLY PERIOD A.D. 33-60	LATER PERIOD A.D. 60-67
Book of Acts	Ephesians—2 Timothy
Tongues mentioned often	Tongues never mentioned
Healings	No healings
Exorcisms	No exorcisms
Raising the dead	No raising of dead

There were certain gifts that were "signs of an apostle" (2 Corinthians 12:12). As we have seen, these included tongues (1 Corinthians 14:22), exorcisms (Matthew 10:8), raising the dead (Matthew 10:8), and healing "every disease and sickness" (Matthew 10:1). During the time of "the Acts of the Apostles" these were all done freely (Acts 2-6, 8-10, 16, 19, 28). Indeed, Paul was still exercising his gifts in the last chapter of Acts (28:9) around A.D. 58. Likewise, these same gifts are mentioned in the Epistles (1 Corinthians 12, 14) referring to events that happened during this period (A.D. 33–60).

However, as soon as we arrive at the time of Paul's imprisonments (around A.D. 60-67) there is not only a complete absence of reference to any of these special apostolic gifts (see Appendix 8), there is strong evidence that they no longer possessed these abilities. For example, the same apostle who could heal everyone on a whole island (Acts 28:9) could no longer even heal his coworkers in the ministry. The apostles could heal a person born lame (Acts 3), but Paul could not give Timothy miraculous relief from a simple stomach ailment and had to recommend that he take medicine for it (1 Timothy 5:23). The same apostle who exorcised a demon on command (Acts 15) could only hope for repentance that Hymenaeus and Philetus would "escape from the trap of the devil" (2 Timothy 2:26). And the same apostle who once had the power to raise the dead (Acts 20) now cannot even raise his needed friend Trophimus from a sick bed (2 Timothy 4:20). And when we reach Hebrews (A.D. 68–69) the sign gifts are referred to as a past event (2:3-4). The writer says that what Jesus announced *"was confirmed to us by those who heard him* [apostles]. God also testified to it by signs, wonders and various miracles."

Even a casual observer can see that there is a marked contrast between the free exercise of sign gifts in the earlier period with their stark absence in the later period. Indeed, the very gifts that distinguished an apostle, such as, raising the dead, healing incurable diseases, exorcising demons on command, and speaking in unknown foreign languages, are no longer expressed in the later period. They have ceased, just as Paul predicted they would (1 Corinthians 13:8).*

---

*Although Paul does not specify here when these gifts would cease, he does say that they will. Furthermore, he hints that this would occur as the church progressed toward "maturity" (1 Corinthians 13:10; cf. Ephesians 4:12). Although this will not be complete till the Second Coming (v. 12), he does not say that all the gifts will last until then. Indeed, it is obvious from the contrasts above that the gifts petered out as the early church matured.

Sorting out the Genuine Gifts from the Counterfeit

There are no apostles today, so there are no special signs of
an apostle. If there were apostles, then there would be new
revelation from apostles. But apostolic revelation is divinely
authoritative and infallible. It is on the same level as the
Holy Scriptures (2 Peter 3:15-16). If such revelations existed
today, they would be as authoritative as the Bible. For since
they would come from God they would have the same divine,
infallible, and inerrant authority the Bible has (see Appendix 3). Few who believe these gifts exist are willing to carry
through consistently the logic of their position.

Are There New Revelations Today? Many today claim to be
receiving visions, dreams, and revelations from God. The
problem is that their "revelations" are not infallible. Some of
them are flatly wrong. But a fallible revelation from God is a
contradiction in terms (see Appendix 3). A few examples of
present-day "revelations" will illustrate the point. In April
1973 David Wilkerson prophesied on the basis of a vision he
had, warning that "more than one-third of the United States
will be designated a disaster area within the next few years"
(Wilkerson 1974, 35). He added, "There is not the slightesт
doubt in my mind about this forthcoming massive earthquake on our continent" (p. 32). He saw his vision as a fulfillment of Joel's prophesy that young men would see visions in
the last days (p. 13), placing himself in continuity with biblical prophets (see also pp. 7-9).

There is one thing fundamentally wrong with this amazing
and precise prophecy of David Wilkerson—it never happened. He said it would certainly happen within "the next
few years," but it did not. It is now fifteen years later, and no
such earthquake occurred. It is abundantly clear that "few
years" cannot mean over fifteen for three reasons.

First, it is contrary to the ordinary meaning of "few" to take
it as more than a handful of years or so. Second, Wilkerson
says in another place in the same book that his prophecies do
not apply to the period beyond a decade. Beyond a decade he
does not claim certainty but has "only a hazy glimpse." But
Wilkerson claimed to be without "the slightest doubt" about
this prediction about the earthquake (p. 32). Third, else-

where in the same book he defines "a good long while," as the time one should keep a car before trading it. But if the time to keep a car (say, ten or fifteen years) is "a good long while," then a "few" years is certainly going to be five or more at most. But it is already fifteen years since Wilkerson made the prophecy of which he claimed to be certain.

Other contemporary "prophets" have had similar difficulties with fulfillments. Noted TV evangelist Pat Robertson predicted that the stock market would crash. In his own words, "I was praying one day in 1969, and the Lord spoke plainly to my inner man: 'The stock market is going to crash.' Then he added, 'Only the securities of our government will be safe'" (Robertson 1984, 193). As everyone knows the stock market did not crash, and there have been a lot of other safe investments for years since then.

The problem with making testable prophecies in the name of the Lord is that they might prove to be false. This might not seem to be too significant until we remember that the test of a prophet is not whether he is sometimes right but whether he is ever wrong. Moses declared: "If what a prophet proclaims in the name of the LORD does not take place or come true, that is a message the LORD has not spoken. That prophet has spoken presumptuously" (Deuteronomy 18:22). The penalty for false prophecy under the Old Testament Law was death (v. 20). If that law were still in effect today, there would undoubtedly be far fewer persons claiming prophetic powers.

Listen to the testimony of a former charismatic pastor about the gift of "prophecy" he and his church exercised:

I loved speaking in tongues. And in the face of mounting evidence which contradicted the validity of my own experiences, I did everything in my power to hold fast. I searched the Scriptures. I prayed. I practiced these gifts more than many. But eventually, the gap between my experience of these gifts and their portrayal in Scripture stretched my sense of integrity to the limits. (Babcox 1985, 67)

The Bible says that only apostles had or could give these special gifts, and apostles lived only in the first century.

When the apostles and those to whom they gave these gifts died, then these special miraculous signs ceased as well.

Miraculous Confirmation of Apostles. Apostles not only received special revelations from God, but they also received special confirmations as well. There was a sign to confirm the sermon, a miracle to attest to their message. For "salvation which was first announced by the Lord, was confirmed to us by those who heard him. God also testified to it by signs, wonders and various miracles" (Hebrews 2:3-4).

The pattern of divine confirmation has been the same down through the ages. Whenever God commissions a prophet to speak for Him, He gives miraculous confirmation of that prophet to those who need it. God did this for Moses (Exodus 4), for Elijah (1 Kings. 18), for Jesus (Acts 2:2), and for the apostles (Hebrews 2:3-4). So anyone speaking as an apostle or prophet today must show the special signs of an apostle (2 Corinthians 12:12). And if apostles exist today, then their revelations are just as divinely authoritative and infallible as those in the Bible.

What were the unique qualifications of an apostle, and how do we know that apostles and new apostolic revelations do not exist today?

First, an apostle was an eyewitness of the resurrected Christ (Acts 1:22; 1 Corinthians 9:1). Only those who were alive in the first century qualify. Anyone who claims to be an apostle today would have to be nearly two thousand years old.

Second, an apostle could and did perform miraculous and instantaneous healings of organic sicknesses. Peter healed the man born crippled "and instantly the man's feet and ankles became strong. He jumped to his feet and began to walk" (Acts 3:7-8). The Scriptures add that "everyone was filled with awe, and many wonders and miraculous signs were done by the apostles" (Acts 2:43). We read that "the apostles performed many miraculous signs and wonders among the people" (Acts 5:12). So impressive were these supernatural healings that "crowds gathered also from the towns around Jerusalem, bringing their sick and those tormented by evil spirits, and all of them were healed" (5:16). In fact, there is not a single case of attempted healing that failed. Paul healed everyone on the island of Malta, for when news of one of his healings spread, "the rest of the sick on the island came and were cured" (Acts 28:9).

Third, apostles could and did convey supernatural powers on others. The first deacons were chosen and presented to the "apostles, who prayed and laid their hands on them." Then "Stephen . . . did great wonders and miraculous signs among the people" (Acts 6:6, 8). Another deacon the apostles laid hands on had miraculous powers. The Bible says "the crowds heard Philip and saw the miraculous signs he did . . ." (Acts 8:6). Timothy was given his gifts by the laying on of the hands of the apostle Paul (2 Timothy 1:6). So the apostles not only had special miraculous powers, but they also had the special ability to convey these gifts on others who worked with them in establishing the universal church (Ephesians 2:20). And once the foundation was laid in the apostles' teaching (Acts 2:22) and recorded in the New Testament, there was no need for these sign gifts.

Fourth, the apostles raised the dead. Jesus commanded the apostles to raise the dead (Matthew 10:1). Jesus raised the dead on several occasions (Luke 7, 8; John 11). And the apostles also raised the dead (Acts 9, 20). These were people who had truly died physically, not people who had fainted or were in a coma. In the case of Lazarus he had been dead for four days, and his body had begun to decompose (John 11:39). Some claim to be able to raise the dead today, but they usually refuse to give names and addresses.

When specifics are given about alleged resurrections from the dead and the details are checked, the evidence is lacking that the person was actually dead. This is the case with the so-called "resurrections" from Indonesia (Peters 1973). And John Wimber gives no specifics of the claimed resurrections in his book (Wimber 1987, 38, 62). A few people even claim to be able to resurrect the dead. Most of the cases are either based on hearsay evidence or else there is no real evidence the person was physically dead. The few cases where specifics are given turn out to be people who had fainted or were in a coma. No one is bringing them back from the graves (see chapter 8).

Fifth, as we have seen, the apostles spoke in real languages they had never learned, and those that spoke those native tongues could understand (Acts 2:1-8). There is no evidence that anyone has this supernatural gift today. Even most charismatics do not claim to be able to speak in a real knowable language. Rather, they claim to speak in a private tongue or so-called prayer language. This could be considered spiritual groanings. It is an attempt to utter the unutterable that comes out as unintelligible. It is a kind of spiritual stuttering. These utterances should not be confused with the supernatural gift of speaking in a foreign language that the apostles exercised in Acts 2 (see Appendix 5).

We can clearly distinguish what many call "the gift of tongues" today from the special supernatural gift of speaking in a foreign language that was experienced by early Christians throughout the Book of Acts. This New Testament gift of a real language was a supernatural power that they were given instantly. It was not something they were taught to do, nor was it nonlanguage utterances. The gift of foreign languages the apostles experienced was truly supernatural.

There is no evidence that anyone today has a supernatural gift to speak in a real language to which he was never exposed. The few instances offered in which a real language, unknown to the speaker, is used are generally not scrutinized critically. For example, these questions are not carefully explored.

1. Can it be demonstrated that the person is speaking a real language, not simply linguistic gibberish?
2. Can it be demonstrated that the person was exposed to the foreign words, phrases, or sentences that he used at another time in his life so that he is being activated in a manner similar to memory activation while under hypnosis?
3. Does the person do this repeatedly so that it can be considered an abiding gift? Or was the alleged occasion of speaking in a real foreign language an isolated instance? For a sudden, one-time utterance in a real unlearned language would only qualify for a miracle in *fact* but not as an abiding *gift*.

The current claim to possess the New Testament gifts, such as the apostles exercised in the Book of Acts, remains without confirmation. And since the New Testament clearly limits this special powers to the apostles and limits the apostles to the first century, we must conclude that these apostolic sign gifts do not exist today. The difference can be illustrated as follows.

MIRACLES

GIFT OF	FACT OF
In Bible times	At any time
Some humans had it	No human has it
Done only through human agents	Done without using human agents
Confirms new revelation	Does not confirm new revelation
Temporary	Permanent

Summary

The apostles possessed unique gifts, including instantaneous healings of organic sickness, speaking in real but unknown (to them) foreign languages, and even raising people who were actually physically dead. It is apparent from the nature of these gifts that no one possesses them today.

Of course, God still performs miracles, but no one has the gift of miracles. But this should not seem strange, for neither does anyone have the gift of apostleship today. God does not change, but His plan for different times has changed. God once required animal sacrifices but no longer does. God once gave new, normative revelation for the church, but both charismatics and noncharismatics agree that He no longer does. So it should not seem strange that God no longer performs miracles with the purpose of confirming new revelation, which He is no longer giving.

God still intervenes from time to time for His own glory. But since He has already confirmed the revelation that He gave to the apostles as the foundation of the church, He has no need to give special sign gifts to confirm new revelation. Jesus is the full and final revelation of God. "In the past God spoke to our forefathers through the prophets, . . . but in these last days he has spoken to us by his Son" (Hebrews 1:1). And this revelation of Christ "was confirmed to us by those who heard him [apostles]. God also testified to it by signs, wonders and various miracles" (Hebrews 2:3-4).

This full and final revelation of Christ through the apostles is preserved in the twenty-seven books of the New Testament. So the Bible is God's full and final revelation for believers today. As Christian creeds and confessions say, "The Bible is sufficient for faith and practice." Hence, the Christian motto today should be: "The word of God, nothing more, nothing less, and nothing else." It is an insult to the sufficiency and finality of Holy Scripture to claim it is God's full and final revelation only to set it aside and ask God to speak directly to us. For the Spirit of God who inspired the Word of God (2 Timothy 3:16) used it to speak to the people of God. God does not bypass His Word to speak to His people.

Those who claim that only through "power evangelism" of signs and wonders will the masses believe the message of the Bible need to be reminded of the words of our Lord: "If they do not listen to Moses and the prophets, they will not be convinced even if someone rises from the dead" (Luke 16:31). Further, as one scholar insightfully noted,

This thesis is disproved in Jesus' public ministry. His greatest miracle was calling Lazarus out of the tomb after he had been dead for four days. But instead of acknowledging Him as Messiah, the Pharisees who witnessed the miracle began plotting together to kill Him (John 11:38-53)." (Sarles 1986, 80)

Indeed, Jesus condemned the sign-seekers of His day, saying, "A wicked and adulterous generation asks for a miraculous sign!" (Matthew 12:39). We should not be seeking signs for their own sake, but the Savior. Our Great Commission to unbelievers is not centered in physical healing but in spiritual deliverance (Matthew 28:18-20). True power evangelism stresses the power of the message, not the power of miracles.

POWER EVANGELISM

BIBLICAL	UNBIBLICAL
Proclaim Savior	Perform signs
Spiritual healing	Physical healing
Power of message	Power of "miracles"
Focus on His miracles	Focus on our "miracles"

Appendix 1. Miracles and the Element of Faith

Miracles where faith of recipient was present

1. Healing a lame man (John 5:1-9)
2. Cleansing a leper (Matthew 8:2-4; Mark 1:40-45; Luke 5:12-16)
3. Healing a man with a withered hand (Matthew 12:9-13; Mark 3:1-5; Luke 6:6-10)
4. Healing a man born blind (John 9:1-7)
5. Healing blind Bartimaeus (Matthew 20:29-34; Mark 10:46-52; Luke 18:35-43)
6. Healing a hemorrhaging woman (Matthew 9:20-22; Mark 5:25-34; Luke 8:43-48)
7. Cleansing ten lepers (Luke 17:11-19)
8. Peter walking on water (Matthew 14:24-33)
9. First miraculous catch of fish (Luke 5:1-11)
10. Second miraculous catch of fish (John 21:1-11)

Miracles without faith of recipient present

1. Healing a nobleman's son (John 4:46-54)
2. Delivering a demoniac (Mark 1:23-28; Luke 4:31-36)
3. Healing a paralytic (Matthew 9:2-8; Mark 2:3-12; Luke 5:18-26)
4. Healing a centurion's servant (Matthew 8:5-13; Luke 7:1-10)
5. Healing a blind and mute man (Matthew 12:22; Luke 11:14)
6. Delivering demoniacs of Gadara (Matthew 8:28-34; Mark 5:1-20; Luke 8:26-39)
7. Delivering a deaf-mute demoniac (Matthew 9:32-33)
8. Multiplying loaves and fish for five thousand (Matthew 14:14-21; Mark 6:34-44; Luke 9:12-17; John 6:5-13)
9. Multiplying loaves and fish for four thousand (Matthew 15:29-31; Mark 8:1-9)
10. Delivering the Syrophoenician's daughter (Matthew 15:21-28; Mark 7:24-30)
11. Healing a deaf mute in Decapolis (Mark 7:31-37)
12. Delivering a demon-possessed boy (Matthew 17:14-18; Mark 9:14-29; Luke 9:38-42)
13. Restoring Malchus's ear (Luke 22:49-51; John 18:10)
14. Walking on water (Matthew 14:24-33; Mark 6:45-52; John 6:16-21)
15. Healing two blind men (Matthew 9:27-31)

16. Healing a man with dropsy (Luke 14:1-4)
17. Healing a crippled woman on the Sabbath (Luke 13:10-17)
18. Healing a blind man (Mark 8:22-26)

Miracles where faith of recipient could not be present

1. Turning water to wine (John 2:1-11)
2. Raising a widow's son (Luke 7:11-15)
3. Calming the sea (Matthew 8:18-27; Mark 4:35-41; Luke 8:22-25)
4. Raising Jairus's daughter (Matthew 9:18-26; Mark 5:22-43; Luke 8:41-56)
5. Raising Lazarus (John 11:17-44)
6. Cursing the fig tree (Matthew 21:18-19; Mark 11:12-14)
7. Finding tax money in a fish (Matthew 17:24-27)

Miracles where unbelief was present

1. Healing the sick in Nazareth (Mark 6:5)
2. Resurrection appearance to Thomas (John 20:25-29)
3. Resurrection appearance to James (1 Corinthians 15:7; John 7:5)
4. Resurrection appearance to Jude (John 7:5; 1 Corinthians 15:6; Jude 1)
5. Delivering demon-possessed boy (Matthew 17:14-18; Mark 9:14-29; Luke 9:38-42)

Appendix 2. Are Miracles Always Successful, Immediate, and Permanent?

Are Miracles Always Successful?

Unbelief in Nazareth (Mark 6:4-5). One of the characteristics of genuine miracles is that they are always successful (see chapter 2). One apparent exception to this is found in Mark 6:5, which says, "He could not do any miracles there, except lay his hands on a few sick people and heal them" (Mark 6:5). At first glance this verse seems to contradict the idea that Jesus was always successful in performing miracles. However, under closer examination the apparent contradiction disappears. It states that Jesus did not do any miracles there except a few healings. The text does not say, nor does it imply, that Jesus attempted to perform a miracle and failed.

Nor does this verse say that Jesus tried to heal some but was unsuccessful because of their unbelief. It was not that it was impossible for Jesus to do miracles there, but simply that it was not desirable. Matthew says very clearly that Jesus "did not do many miracles there because of their lack of faith" (Matthew 13:58).

Furthermore, the text states clearly that Jesus did perform some miracles there for He laid "his hands on a few sick and healed them" (Mark 6:5). Yet because of those who did not believe, Jesus found it morally impossible to exercise His power. He never "cast his pearls before swine." Jesus refused to force Himself upon those who had rejected Him. This fits the character of God revealed elsewhere. For Jesus would not force the unwilling Jews into His flock (Matthew 23:37).

The Demon-possessed Boy (Matthew 17:14-21). Jesus gave His apostles the power to cast out demons (Matthew 10:1). However, there is a case where they were apparently unsuccessful in delivering a boy from a demon. The boy with demonic seizures was brought to the disciples, "but they could not heal him" (Matthew 17:16). Indeed, the disciples asked Jesus, "Why couldn't we drive it out?" (v. 19). Jesus' response was that they did not have faith, even the smallest amount like a grain of mustard seed (vv. 20-21).

Is this story a case of a miracle that failed? Not really; it is simply an indication that even gifts from God will not work unless they are faithfully exercised. First of all, the miracle did not fail. Jesus cast out the demon "and he was healed from that moment" (v. 18).

Second, the disciples could also have healed him immediately if they had used their gift of exorcism and simply commanded the demon to depart. It was not a matter of possessing great faith to do this. Jesus said to them emphatically that if they would exercise even the smallest amount of faith that "nothing will be impossible for them" (v. 21). The disciples simply forgot for the moment to faithfully exercise the power that Jesus had already given them.

Finally, contrary to the claim of faith healers today, it was not the lack of faith on the part of the recipient that hindered the healing (see Appendix 1). If it was a lack in anyone's faith, it was failure of the disciples. God's gifts do not work automatically or mechanically (2 Kings 4:29-31). Nor do they work like magic (Acts 19:13f.). The recipient of the gift must faithfully exercise the gift. The disciples did not do this. Jesus rebuked them and did it immediately, as the disciples should have done it.

The Sickness of Epaphroditus (Philippians 2:25-27). Paul informs us that his fellow worker Epaphroditus "was ill, and almost died" (Philippians 2:27). But this is strange if the apostle had the gift of healing that never failed. Is this not an example of a healing by an apostle that failed? Here again the answer is no for several reasons. First of all, there is no record that Paul ever attempted to heal Epaphroditus and failed. It simply says he was deathly sick. Second, it is possible that Paul no longer possessed the gift of healing at this time. When he wrote Ephesians, Paul listed no such gift. We know that a few years later Paul told Timothy to take medicine for his ailment (1 Timothy 5:23) and "left Trophimus at Miletum sick" (2 Timothy 4:20). At any rate, there is not the slightest indication in the text that anyone with the divine gift of healing failed in an attempt to heal Epaphroditus or anyone else.

The Case of the Seven Spirits Returning (Matthew 12:43-45). Jesus said, "When an evil spirit comes out of a man, . . . it goes and takes with it seven other spirits more wicked than itself, and they go in and live there" (Matthew 12:43-45). Some have taken this as an example of a miracle of exorcism that failed. However, this conclusion is unfounded for several reasons.

First, the text does not say that this demon was exorcised by Christ or an apostle. It may have simply been an illustration used by Christ. Even if it represents an actual event, it does not say the demon was ever cast out. It simply says it "came out." There are other ways than an immediate exorcism that a demon can leave, namely, by simply withdrawing on its own or by a ministry of deliverance through prayer.

Second, Jewish priests also drove out demons (Acts 19:13). So this spirit could have been driven out by those other than Jesus or His disciples. In fact, Jesus states that there are many who claim to cast out demons in His name that were never His disciples (Matthew 7:22).

Third, Jewish exorcists were not always successful. In fact, when they tried to cast out demons once in Jesus' name, the demonic man overpowered them and they failed (Acts 19:14-16). Finally, when Jesus said to them that "a kingdom cannot be divided against itself" (Matthew 12:26), He did not mean that it was impossible for those in league with the Devil to cast out demons. He did not mean that it is a contradiction in itself for a kingdom to have inner conflicts, but only that it must be unified in relation to others who oppose it. In other words, since Satan's kingdom was unified in its opposition to Christ (their foe), then they could not consistently ascribe

His miracles to the work of Beelzebub, the prince of the demons (Matthew 12:27). If Satan is the source of the demonic invasion into a life, then there is no reason he could not call off his "troops" for a time if it suited his overall plans of deception.

The Case of Jesus Repeatedly Commanding a Demon to Depart. Mark 5:8 says Jesus "had been saying [imperfect tense] to him, 'Come out of the man, you unclean spirit!'" This can be translated, "Jesus had repeatedly said." If this is the case, then it would seem to be an exception to the rule that a miracle always has an immediate response. For if it did, then it would seem to be unnecessary to repeat the command.

However, this may be pressing a point of grammar too far for several reasons. First, the text can be translated simply, as the NIV does, "he had said to him" just before they cried out.

Second, even if it is insisted that some kind of continual activity in the past is implied in Jesus' command, it could be translated, "he was in the process of saying to him" when he interrupted and pled not to be tormented (v. 7; cf. Luke 8:28).

Third, even the demon's plea "If [ei] you drive us out, send us into the herd of pigs" (Matthew 8:31) means in Greek that he knew immediately that he would be sent out.

Fourth, from the very moment Jesus issued the command to depart there was never a question as to whether they would go but simply *where* they would go—to the Pit ("abyss") or into the pigs (Matthew 8:31-32).

Fifth, the command to depart ("Come out") is in the aorist tense, calling for a decisive response (Mark 5:8; Luke 8:29).

Finally, immediate need not mean "that very instant." The few minutes delay in execution of Jesus' command may have been to respond to their plea not to be tormented. At any rate, Jesus' command was promptly obeyed, and the demon departed.

Are Miracles Always Immediate? (Mark 8:22-25)

Another characteristic of miracles is that the results were always immediate. There is no account of a healing which occurred over a period of days or even hours. However, one event that appears to have involved a short time is recorded in Mark 8:22-26, where Jesus healed a blind man in two stages. Jesus first anointed his eyes, and the man immediately began to see, but only dimly. Then Jesus put His hands on the man's eyes, and immediately "he saw everything clearly" (8:25).

It is plain enough that this healing was in two stages, but it certainly was not a gradual healing. Each stage was immediate and complete. The whole process probably took no more than a very few minutes. Furthermore, the context of this event sheds some possible light on the reason why Jesus may have performed this miraculous healing in two stages.

Jesus had just fed the five thousand, and yet the disciples lacked faith. Their condition led to some of the most severely rebuking questions that Jesus ever directed to His disciples. This series of questions was designed to lead them to recognize the spiritual lessons which should have been gained in the miraculous feeding that had just occurred. Mark ends this passage with one of Jesus' questions to the disciples, "Do you still not understand?" (8:21).

Following this severe rebuke was the encounter with the blind man whom Jesus healed in two stages. The first stage was illustrative of the condition of His disciples. Although Jesus had given them spiritual sight, they could not yet see clearly. However, just as Jesus would again touch the blind man to restore his sight perfectly, so the disciples could find comfort in the fact that Jesus would also continue to touch their lives until they could see "everything clearly."

Although Jesus could have healed the blind man in one stage, He may have chosen to use this opportunity to teach and comfort the disciples after His severe rebuke of them. The two stage healing may have been an object lesson for them in their spiritual growth. When Jesus spit on the man's eyes, immediately his sight returned. Though his sight was not perfectly clear, it nevertheless had returned immediately. The second stage was just as immediate. When Jesus touched his eyes again, immediately his sight became perfectly clear.

This miracle involved no period of gradual improving of the eyes. Rather, each stage was an instantaneous step toward total restoration. The degree of restoration achieved in each step was Jesus' goal. He did not attempt to restore the man's sight completely in the first stage. His desire was not only to heal but also to teach. To accomplish this He immediately brought about the results of each stage that would provide the lesson His disciples needed.

In summation, this passage does not contradict the principle of immediacy; it simply gives two steps of immediate healing. This emphasizes the immediacy all the more. The fact remains that nowhere in the Scriptures is there an account of a gradual healing stretching over a period of days or hours. When Jesus healed, the results were always immediate.

Are Miracles Always Permanent? (John 11)

As we examined the miracles of healing in the Bible, we found that the Bible does not record a single case of relapse. However, some have charged that Lazarus's eventual death is an exception, for his resurrection was not permanent; he relapsed at his eventual death. Before we can answer this objection we must provide a definition of what is meant by a relapse. To relapse means to slip or fall back into a former condition, especially after improvement or seeming improvement.

After Jesus had raised Lazarus from the dead, it can be safely assumed that eventually Lazarus died. Was this a relapse? Had Jesus cured Lazarus of all eventual death? Obviously not. Jesus had simply restored Lazarus to his mortal life. Lazarus did not receive his permanent resurrection body. We must "wait eagerly" for this (Romans 8:23). At the resurrection our bodies will be raised and never be subject to death again (1 Corinthians 15:51-55). Lazarus must wait for this with the rest of believers.

The fact that Lazarus was only restored to his mortal life cannot be considered a relapse. Lazarus was never given an immortal body and then returned to a mortal one. Rather, he was restored to his prior mortal body, which eventually was going to die anyway. Since, unlike the resurrection of Christ, Lazarus's restoration to life was not a cure from eventual death, it was expected that he would eventually die. When he did die, it was not a relapse of the miracle of his raising any more than all the other miracles of healing can be called failures because the persons healed all eventually died. The miracle of Lazarus's raising was just as perfect and permanent as any other healing; it lasted his whole lifetime.

Appendix 3. Is the New Testament Gift of Prophecy Fallible?

Arguments for the Fallibility of New Testament Prophecy

Some claim that the New Testament gift of prophecy was not infallible. In other words, they believe that some of a New Testament prophet's utterances could be wrong. In support of this view they offer the following arguments.

1. *Agabus's prediction about Paul was wrong.* Agabus predicted that Paul would be bound and handed over to the Gentiles if he went to Jerusalem (Acts 21:10). He tried to no avail to persuade Paul not to go to Jerusalem. This they take as proof that Agabus's prophecy was wrong.

2. *One prophet could interrupt another.* According to 1 Corinthians 14:30 one prophet could interrupt another when he was giving a prophecy. But they insist that if it was really God speaking, then the utterance could not be interrupted.

3. *The audience was to judge the prophecy being given.* Paul said the people receiving the prophecy should judge or "weigh carefully what is said" (v. 29). But they claim that there would be no reason for it to be judged by the audience if it was infallible.

4. *There was no "Thus says the Lord" with it.* Another reason given for holding that the New Testament prophecies were fallible is that those uttering them did not accompany their statements with the "Thus says the Lord" used by Old Testament prophets. So they insist that the New Testament

prophets were not placing their utterances on the same level as those in the Old Testament.

Response to the Arguments for the Fallibility of New Testament Prophecy

1. *Agabus's prophecy was not false.* Agabus predicted that "the Jews of Jerusalem will bind the owner of this belt [Paul] and will hand him over to the Gentiles" (Acts 21:11). And that is literally what happened. Later in the same chapter we read that "some Jews . . . stirred up the whole crowd and seized him" (v. 27). And when "the Roman troops" came "they stopped beating Paul." Then they relinquished Paul to the "commander [who] came up and arrested him and ordered him to be bound with two chains" (vv. 31-33). When the Jews seized Paul, it would have been natural to restrain him by binding him just as the prophecy had indicated (v. 11). Thus the prophecy was fulfilled as stated in the same chapter.

2. *Interrupting a prophecy does not mean it was not of God* The fact that prophets could be interrupted does not imply that their message was not from God. Rather, it reveals that "the spirits of prophets are subject to the control of prophets" (1 Corinthians 14:32). Ecstatic utterances were common among pagans, such as the Corinthians once were. In these occult prophecies the one giving the utterances was overpowered by the spirit giving the utterance. By contrast, Paul is saying that if a revelation is truly from God, then the prophet will remain in conscious control of his mind and will. In short, if it is really of God, it can wait. Paul was saying, "Take your turn." For "God is not a God of disorder but of peace" (v. 33).

3. *Judging the prophecy does not imply the gift of prophecy is fallible.* The New Testament believers were told to judge or weigh what was being offered as a prophecy. This does not imply that a true prophet could give a false prophecy, but that false prophets could pretend to give true utterances. Jesus warned that "many false prophets will appear and deceive many people" (Matthew 24:11). John the apostle urged Christians not to "believe every spirit, but test the

spirits to see whether they are from God, because many false prophets have gone out into the world" (1 John 4:1). So the reason New Testament believers were to "judge" the utterances was not because a true prophet could give a false prophecy but because there were false prophets.

4. *The formula "Thus says the Lord" is not essential.* Many Old Testament prophets did not use the phrase "Thus says the Lord." Some prophets before Christ simply said "I saw" [in a vision] or "the Lord showed me" (see Amos 7:1; 8:1). Others just spoke with authority without any formula (as David did in the Psalms). Furthermore, when Agabus made his prediction he did use a formula indicating it was from God, just as many Old Testament prophets did. He said, "the Holy Spirit says, . . ." (Acts 21:11). So there is no reason to believe that New Testament prophets exercised their gifts any differently than did prophets in the Old Testament.

Arguments Showing That the New Testament Gift of Prophecy Was the Same as That in the Old Testament

1. *New Testament prophets were in continuity with their Old Testament predecessors.* The Old Testament predicted the prophet John the Baptist (Malachi 3:5). Jesus declared that John was the greatest of the prophets (Matthew 11:11), thus placing him in line with the Old Testament prophets. John the apostle spoke of "the prophecy of this book [of Revelation]" that he wrote (Revelation 22:7). And the angel from God that spoke to him placed him among "the prophets" such as the other "servants" God used in the Old Testament (22:6). And John said of himself, "I am a fellow servant with . . . the prophets" (22:9). So from John the Baptist to John the apostle, New Testament prophets stood in continuity with Old Testament prophets. And their revelations from God were both authoritative and infallible (see Revelation 22:18-19).

2. *New Testament prophets were placed along with apostles as the foundation of the church.* According to Ephesians 2:20, the church is "built on the foundation of the apostles and prophets, with Christ Jesus himself as the chief cornerstone." That it is a reference to New Testament prophets is

evident from two facts. First of all, the order of listing would have been prophets and apostles if he had been referring to Old Testament prophets. But each time the phrase occurs it is always "apostles and prophets" (see 3:5). Second, Paul affirms clearly that the Old Testament prophets did not understand "the mystery of Christ, which was not made known to men in other generations as it has now been revealed by the Spirit to God's holy apostles and prophets." And in the parallel passage in Colossians Paul says plainly that "the mystery . . . has been kept hidden for ages and generations, but is now disclosed to the saints" (Colossians 1:26).

So the New Testament prophets, along with the apostles, were the means through which God revealed Himself to the church in the New Testament times. But the apostles' revelations were divinely authoritative and infallible (see 1 Corinthians 14:37). It follows, then, that the New Testament prophets gave equally authoritative and infallible messages. If they did not, then the church is built on some fallible prophecy, since it is "built on the foundation of the apostles and prophets." That is, they are the foundation of the church. They established it. Indeed, many of the New Testament books were not written by apostles (Mark, Luke, Acts, Hebrews, James, and Jude). If their prophetic utterances are not infallible, then it would follow that their books are not infallible, as are the other New Testament books written by apostles.

3. *The New Testament prophets received "revelations" from God.* Paul describes what a New Testament prophet received as a "revelation" from God (1 Corinthians 14:29). This is the same word used to describe his own words from God in the same book (1 Corinthians 2:10). Indeed, Paul speaks of these as "words taught by the Spirit" (2:13). But the Holy Spirit is the Spirit of truth, and the Spirit of truth cannot utter error. "It is impossible for God to lie" (Hebrews 6:18). So whenever a New Testament prophet gave a "revelation" from God, it was just as infallible and without error as were those of the Old Testament prophets or New Testament apostles. God cannot speak fallible words. So if it was a

revelation from God, then it must have been infallible. A
fallible revelation is a contradiction in terms!

4. *New Testament prophets gave predictive prophecies
too.* Foretelling the future was not unique to Old Testament
prophets. The New Testament prophet Agabus "through the
Spirit predicted that a severe famine would spread over the
entire Roman world." Luke adds, "This happened during the
reign of Claudius" (Acts 11:28). When Agabus gave his
prophecy about Paul he declared, "the Holy Spirit says"
(Acts 21:11). So he not only gave predictive prophecies, as
Old Testament prophets did, but he claimed the same divine
authority they did. Hence, if the utterances of Old Testament
prophets were infallible, then so were those of New Testament prophets. And of Old Testament prophets the Bible
declares that if they ever gave a false prophecy that proves
they were not true prophets (Deuteronomy 18:22).

5. *Prophecy is given a high status on the list of gifts.* Prophecy is placed on the New Testament list of gifts, alongside of
apostleship (1 Corinthians 12:28-29) and "miraculous powers" (12:10). Even though both prophecy and tongues were
gifts through which God spoke, Paul listed prophecy above
tongues (1 Corinthians 14:18). He urged the church as a
whole to desire "especially the gift of prophecy" (1 Corinthians 14:1). He said prophecy is a gift by which one gives a
"revelation" from God (14:6). This exalted position Paul
gives to the gift of prophecy is further indication that it is
neither fallible nor inferior to the gift of prophecy in the Old
Testament.

Both Old and New Testament prophecies were means by
which the infallible word of God was given to the people of
God. As David described it, "the Spirit of the Lord spoke
through me; his word was on my tongue" (2 Samuel 23:2). In
brief, the prophets words were Gods words. What the prophet said, God said. As the Apostle Peter noted, "prophecy
never had its origin in the will of man, but men spoke from
God as they were carried along by the Holy Spirit" (2 Peter
1:21).

It follows from this that either those who claim the gift of prophecy today are uttering infallible truths on a par with those in the Bible or else the New Testament gift of prophecy does not exist today. For the "prophecies" given today are not infallible, but are often false. Thus, we must conclude that the New Testament gift of prophecy does not exist today. What is being called "the gift of prophecy" is really no more than preaching. It is authoritative insofar as it is based on God's infallible and inerrant Word. When it deviates from that, it is not authoritative or inerrant.

Appendix 4.
The Miracle of Manna

A natural occurrence is by definition something that happens over and over. Miracles do not. Natural events are regularities; miracles are singularities. If something occurs regularly it is not a miracle (see chapter 3). In view of this description of miracles as a rare, irregular, unique occurrence there is a problem with the miracle of manna in the Old Testament.

God provided manna for the children of Israel daily for forty years (Exodus 16; Numbers 11). It was so regular that they could depend on it each morning. How then can it qualify as a miracle which is an irregular event? In response to this it should be noted that the giving of manna was indeed a miracle, and that even though it occurred repeatedly, nevertheless it was characterized by many irregularities.

First, it was irregular in its object. Only Israel received it (Exodus 16:1f.). Of all the nations in the world God gave manna to only one people—Israel. Natural laws, by contrast, are true for all nations. The law of gravity, for example, does not just apply in the United States. So the singular object of the manna sets it off as unique.

Second, the miracle of manna was irregular in its time. Manna has not fallen at that place or any other place over all of time or even for generations, except during that unique forty year period while Israel was in the wilderness (Exodus 16:35: Joshua 5:12).

Third, the manna was irregular in its occurrence. Manna did not fall every day; it appeared only six days a week (Exodus 16:26-27). None fell on Saturday, their day of rest (v. 27).

Fourth, the miracle of manna was irregular in its amount. It did not come in the same amount each day. Since none fell on Saturday, twice as much fell on Friday (Exodus 16:22). In this way they could have enough to eat for two days (vv. 23-24).

Fifth, the manna was irregular in its duration. The manna that fell every day Sunday through Friday lasted only one day before it spoiled (Exodus 16:20). But the manna that fell on Friday lasted two days so they could have some on Saturday when they could not work (vv. 22-23).

Sixth, the manna was unusual in its preservation. Moses was commanded to put some in a gold jar and place it in the Ark of the Covenant as a testimony (Exodus 16:35; Hebrews 9:4). Although it melted in one day's sun and got maggots (Exodus 16:20), nonetheless it was preserved for generations in a jar without spoiling.

So the miracle of manna was a very irregular event. Even though it happened more often than other miracles, it was irregular like other miracles.

Many other biblical miracles occurred more than once. For example, there are seven raisings from the dead mentioned in Scripture. But the fact that this miracle is repeated does not take away from its uniqueness. Even though it is repeated, nevertheless it is highly irregular for people to rise from the dead. So the manna was highly irregular in its object, time, occurrence, amount, duration, and preservation.

Appendix 5.
Were New Testament
Tongues Real Languages?

Some claim that the gift of tongues spoken of in 1 Corinthians is not the same as that experienced on the day of Pentecost (Acts 2). Tongues at Pentecost were obviously real languages since each one present from the various countries (Acts 2:9-11) heard the apostles speaking "in his own native language" (2:8). However, for various reasons some have argued that the tongues mentioned later in 1 Corinthians are not the same as those spoken in Acts. They believe that the tongues at Corinth were private tongues or prayer languages that do not necessarily have the linguistic pattern of a real language.

Arguments Given in Favor of Private Tongues

Several reasons are offered in support of the "private tongues" view. First, they argue that 1 Corinthians was written later and speaks to a different situation. Second, they contend that Paul speaks of these private tongues as "the tongues of angels" (1 Corinthians 13:1) which are not a known language. Third, they are called "unknown tongues" (1 Corinthians 14:2, 4, King James Version). Fourth, Paul said he spoke "mysteries" (14:2) in his spirit. Fifth, they are called "groans that words cannot express" (Romans 8:26). Sixth, an unknown tongue "does not speak to men but to God; indeed, none understands him" (1 Corinthians 14:2).

A Response to the Arguments in Favor of Private Tongues

First, 1 Corinthians was not written later than Acts; it was written earlier, probably in A.D. 56, while Acts was completed some four years later. Furthermore, the last reference in Acts to tongues (chapter 19) is during the same general time period of the Corinthian church (chapter 18). So there are no grounds for supposing that tongues in Corinth were later and therefore a different experience.

Second, the phrase "tongues of angels" (1 Corinthians 13:1) is probably a figure of speech meaning, "to speak very eloquently." Even if it is taken literally, every time angels spoke in the Bible they spoke in a real language that people could understand (see Genesis 19; Exodus 3; Joshua 5; Judges 13).

Third, the King James translation of the Greek word for "tongues" (*glossolalia*) as "unknown tongues" is misleading. Many readers do not understand that the italicized word *unknown* is not in the original language. Most modern translations correctly omit the word *unknown* because it is not in the Greek.

Fourth, "mysteries" in the Bible are not unintelligible. A biblical "mystery" is something once concealed but now revealed. In fact, Paul speaks of a "mystery" as that of which "I have already written" (Ephesians 3:3). Since he wrote it in Greek, a known language, it is clear that "mystery" here is not an unknown, unintelligible, or inexpressible private language.

Fifth, when Paul speaks of "groans that words cannot express" (Romans 8:26) he is not speaking about tongues. The gift of tongues is nowhere mentioned in this passage or anywhere in Romans, not even in the list of spiritual gifts (Romans 12:6-8). Furthermore, the "groans" of which Paul speaks here "cannot be uttered." But the private tongues are something that people do utter. So they cannot be the same. Finally, the "groans" here are expressed by the Holy Spirit (v. 26); there is no need for the believer to put them in words.

Sixth, Paul says an unknown tongue speaks to God but not to men because unless it is translated, only God can understand it, not because it is basically unintelligible or untranslatable. Indeed, the very fact that He demands that it be interpreted for the church (vv. 10-19) reveals that it is a meaningful language that can be translated.

In addition to the above response to the arguments for "private tongues" in 1 Corinthians there are several other reasons indicating the gift of tongues mentioned in 1 Corinthians is a real or knowable language.

First, as mentioned above, every time tongues appear in Acts they are real languages. It is clear that they were real languages in Acts 2 because each one heard the apostles speaking "in his own native language" (2:8). And Peter declares that the "tongues" in which Cornelius and the Italians spoke in Acts 10 were "the same gift as he gave us" [in Acts 2] (Acts 11:17). And in Acts 19, the only other mention of tongues in Acts, it says that they had the same experience of receiving the Holy Spirit and speaking in tongues. Thus the gift of "tongues" throughout the Book of Acts from chapter 2 (A.D. 33) to the end (A.D. 60) was a real language. Since 1 Corinthians was written during this same time period (A.D. 56) there is no reason to believe that it is anything but a real language.

Second, even within the same context in 1 Corinthians 14 Paul compares tongues to real languages, saying, "There are all sorts of languages in the world, yet none of them is without meaning" (v. 10). It is obvious, then, that he believes the gift of tongues, with which he makes the comparison is, like a real language, something that has meaning.

Third, the fact that the tongues of which Paul spoke in 1 Corinthians could be "interpreted" shows that it was a meaningful language. Otherwise, it would not be an "interpretation" but a creation of the meaning. So the gift of "interpretation" (1 Corinthians 12:30; 14:5, 13) supports the fact that tongues were a real language that could be translated for the benefit of all by this special gift of interpretation.

Fourth, when Paul says "tongues are a sign, not for believers, but for unbelievers" (1 Corinthians 14:22) he quotes the Old Testament (Isaiah 28:11-12) saying, "Through men of strange tongues and through the lips of foreigners I will speak to this people" (v. 21). But the "strange tongues" spoken of here were real languages used by Israel's captors, the Assyrians.

Finally, the positing of a "private language" is suspect

because it is unfalsifiable. There is no way to test it. Further-more, there is nothing unique about them. Anyone can speak in an unintelligible gibberish. People in cults and false religions speak in tongues. Even those who believe in tongues acknowledge that unsaved people have tongues experiences. There is nothing supernatural about them. But there is something unique about speaking complete and meaningful sentences and discourses in a knowable language to which one has never been exposed. This is what the real New Testament gift of tongues entailed. Anything short of this, as "private tongues" are, should not be considered the biblical gift of tongues.

Appendix 6. The Use of Physical Objects in Healing

Many faith healers use physical objects to facilitate cures. Crystals are often used by New Age healers. Some professed Christian healers use prayer cloths, glasses of water, or other religious relics and trinkets. A trained counselor for one famous televangelist asked people to stand on the Bible while she prayed for their healing.

Christian healers appeal to certain passages in the Bible to justify their use of physical objects. First, they claim Moses used a physical rod to perform his miracles (Exodus 4:2f.; 7:1f.). Second, they point to the fact that God spoke through the priestly jewels (the Urim and Thummim) to reveal His will (Exodus 28:30). Third, they note that the Ark of the Covenant was an object protected by supernatural power (1 Samuel 5). Fourth, Jesus once used clay as a means by which He healed a man of blindness (John 9:6f.). Fifth, some people were healed by touching Jesus' garment (Matthew 9:20-22). Sixth, the apostles sent out handkerchiefs by which people were healed (Acts 19:11-12).

There are several significant differences between the use of physical objects in biblical miracles and those used by many famous present-day healers. First, the physical objects through which miracles were performed in the Bible were divinely designated instruments. God told Moses He had appointed the rod "so that they may believe that the Lord . . .

has appeared to you" (Exodus 4:5). Likewise, the Ark of the Covenant was the divinely appointed place where God dwelt (Leviticus 16). Also the Urim and Thummim were designated by God as a means of revealing Himself to His people in special circumstances (Deuteronomy 33:8). Likewise, Jesus put clay on one blind man, but He never appointed it as a means of healing blind people.

Nowhere does God direct that standing on a Bible, drinking prayed-over water, or a crystal be used as a means of healing. These and many more techniques used by healers are humanly contrived but not divinely appointed means for healing.

Second, there is no claim in the Bible that the objects through which God performed miracles had any special power within them. The power of God flowed through them, but it did not reside within them. The physical objects used in the Bible had no inherent power; they were simply the instruments through which God's power was channeled.

Divinely appointed instruments of miracles were conduits of God's miraculous power, but there was no claim to contain within themselves any mystical power of their own. Elisha's staff is a good case in point. When Gehazi tried to use it like a magic wand, laying it on the dead boy, nothing happened (2 Kings 4:31). Only when Elisha came and "prayed to the Lord" was the boy restored to life (vv. 33-35).

The belief that there are special powers resident within certain physical objects like pyramids or crystals is occult in origin, not Christian. It is superstitious, not supernatural. The Bible condemns it as "divination" (Deuteronomy 18:10).

Third, the use of physical objects as a means of miracles in the Bible was under God's control. God not only designated the special objects on the special occasions they were used, but He also decided when they would be used. Samson's long hair is a case in point. When Samson sinned, he lost the power of God that was upon him (Judges 16:20). Not until he was again obedient to God and called upon Him did God again work a miracle through him (Judges 16:28-30). The Bible is very clear that miracles are done only "according to his [God's] will" (Hebrews 2:4). Speaking of spiritual gifts, Paul declared that the Holy Spirit "gives them to each one, just as he determines" (1 Corinthians 12:11).

Miraculous powers are given by God and taken way by Him. He alone controls them. Divine power is not magical. It is not like an Aladdin's lamp that can be rubbed and the genie will appear with the fulfillment of one's wish. It is not a power available for all men to use. Rather, it is a power that uses some men and only some times.

Appendix 7. Did Only Apostles Speak in Tongues at Pentecost?

It is widely held that all 120 in the Upper Room received the gift of tongues on the day of Pentecost. However, the text nowhere says this. In fact, there is good evidence to indicate that the gift of tongues was limited only to apostles or to those to whom they gave the gift. It will be remembered that there were special "signs of an apostle" (2 Corinthians 12:12). The ability to resurrect was one of these unique gifts (Matthew 10:8). Tongues-speaking was another such gift because it was called a "sign" gift (1 Corinthians 14:22). On the day of Pentecost the gift of tongues was apparently given only to the twelve apostles, not to all the disciples. This is supported by the following evidence:

1. Only apostles were promised before Pentecost that "you will be baptized with the Holy Spirit" (Acts 1:5). It is clear from the context that "you" refers only to "the apostles" (v. 2).

2. The "they" (Acts 2:1) on whom the Holy Spirit fell refers back to the previous verse, namely, the "apostles" (1:26).

3. Likewise, "they" and "them" (v. 3) on whom tongues of fire fell refers to the same "apostles."

4. Further, the crowd heard "them" (the same "apostles") speak in tongues (v. 6).

5. Also, those who spoke in tongues were "all . . . Galileans" (2:7), as the apostles were. Even the angel called

them "men of Galilee" (1:11). But the others present in the Upper Room were not all Galileans; some were from Jerusalem and Judea (1:12-14).

6. The group that responded when "they" (2:13) had been accused of drunkenness was "Peter . . . with the eleven" (2:14). This again indicates that those speaking in tongues were the apostles.

7. The fifteen geographical areas listed (2:9-11) probably represent no more than twelve language groups, since some countries spoke the same basic language. So each apostle could have been speaking in one of the languages represented by these countries. Even if there were more than twelve languages represented, some apostles could have spoken in more than one language successively.

8. Since tongues-speaking was one of the special "signs" unique to apostles (1 Corinthians 14:22; 2 Corinthians 12:12), it would not make sense to give it initially to anyone but apostles.

9. Later, whenever anyone received the gift of the Holy Spirit and/or tongues in the early church, it was only through an apostle (Acts 8, 10, 19). Acts 8:18 teaches explicitly that "the Spirit was given at the laying on of the apostles' hands."

10. Supernatural gifts were given in the early church by apostles. For Paul said to Timothy, "Fan into flame the gift of God, which is in you through the laying on of my hands" (2 Timothy 1:6; see 1 Timothy 4:14).

11. Since the church was "built on the foundation of the apostles and prophets" (Ephesians 2:20), the apostles used these special powers to convey supernatural gifts to the leaders of the churches they founded. In this way the early church had an authoritative basis on which to function in the absence of an apostle or written Scripture.

12. Only some were leaders and only some spoke in tongues (1 Corinthians 12:10). Paul said emphatically: "All are not apostles, are they? . . . All do not speak with tongues, do they?" (1 Corinthians 12:29-30, NASB).

Appendix 8. New Testament Lists of Gifts

OPERATION OF SIGN GIFTS

1 Cor. 12, 14	Rom. 12	Eph. 4*	Eph.-2 Tim.
A.D. 56	A.D. 57	A.D. 60	A.D. 60-67
Apostles		Apostles	No gifts listed**
Prophets	Prophecy	Prophets	Paul could not heal:
		Evangelists	Timothy (1 Tim. 5:23)
		Pastor [Teacher]	Epaphroditus (Phil. 2:26)
Teachers	Teaching	[Teachers]?	Trophimus (2 Tim. 4:20)
	Exhortation		
	Leading		
	Serving		
	Giving		
	Mercy		
Miracles			
Healings			
Helps			
Administration			
Tongues			
Interpretation			
Faith			
Knowledge			
Wisdom			
Discerning			
13	7	4(5)	

*The fact that gifts are not listed does not in itself prove that they are not in operation, but when they are not listed in any later list and when there is further evidence they are not in operation (Paul's companions not healed), and they are referred to as past events then this is good evidence the gift is no longer in operation.

**These may be functions, not gifts.

Notes
1. The number of gifts listed decreases with time.
2. Tongues are only in the earliest list.
3. The last two lists have no sign gifts.
4. Last reference to the exercise of a sign gift was around A.D. 58 (Acts 28:9), two years before the end of Acts (v. 30).
5. Beginning with Paul's two imprisonments (A.D. 60-67), Paul lacked the ability to heal even his needed helpers, such as Timothy, Epaphroditus, and Trophimus.
6. By the time of Hebrews (A.D. 68-69) the gifts are referred to as past (2:3-4).

Glossary of Special Terms

magic. Used in two senses: 1) human trickery, illusionism, deception; 2) occult or psychic powers, including demonic powers.

miracle. Used here to describe a divine intervention into nature, a supernatural act of God. As such, a miracle is not simply an unusual or supernormal event (see below). It transcends natural law. Only God can perform miracles, though He sometimes uses human agents.

miraculous. Used broadly of either a miracle (see above) or a supernatural event (see below).

power. One of the three biblical words used to describe a miracle (see also *sign* and *wonder*). *Power* indicates the *source* of the miracle, *wonder* speaks of its *nature*, and *sign* denotes its *purpose* (see Appendix 7).

supernatural. Referring to God. A supernatural act is one that only God can perform. It transcends nature or the laws of nature. All miracles are supernatural acts, but not all supernatural acts are miracles. A miracle is a supernatural act *in* the natural world, whereas other supernatural acts are not visible acts in the physical world, such as the acts of creation or salvation.

supernormal. An unusual but not a supernatural act (see above) that is usually caused by psychic powers, whether human or demonic. It is not a normal event in that it cannot be explained by purely physical causes. Whatever physical forces may be utilized, the real cause is often a superhuman mind or spirit.

sign. One of the biblical words for *miracle*, indicating that it is used to confirm a message or messenger from God. It is to be compared with the other two words for *miracle*: *power* and *wonder*.

wonder. One of the biblical words for miracle pointing to its special nature to attract attention to what God is doing. It should be compared to the other two words for miracle, namely, *sign* and *power* (see above).

Works Cited

Abell, George, and Barry Singer, eds. *Science and the Paranormal*. New York: Scribner's, 1981.

Alexander, Brooks, and David Fetcho, eds. "UFOs: Is Science Fiction Coming True?" *SCP Journal* (Spiritual Counterfeits Project), August 1977.

Alexander, R. H. "Galilee, Sea of," in *The Zondervan Pictorial Encyclopedia of the Bible*. Vol. 2. Merrill C. Tenney, ed. Grand Rapids: Zondervan, 1975.

Asimov, Isaac. "The Genesis War." *Science Digest*, October 1981.

Babcox, Neil. *A Search for Charismatic Reality*. Portland, Ore.: Multnomah, 1985.

Brand, Paul, with Philip Yancey. "A Surgeon's View of Divine Healing." *Christianity Today*, 25 November 1983.

Chryssides, George D. "Miracles and Agents." *Religious Studies* 11 (September 1975).

Clapp, Rodney. "Faith Healing: A Look at What's Happening." *Christianity Today*, 16 December 1983.

———. "One Who Took Up Her Bed and Walked." *Christianity Today*, 16 December 1983.

Cousins, Norman. *Anatomy of an Illness as Perceived by the Patient*. New York: Bantam, 1979.

Eareckson, Joni, and Steve Estes. *A Step Further*. Grand Rapids: Zondervan, 1978.

Edgar, Thomas. *Miraculous Gifts: Are They for Today?* Neptune, N.J.: Loizeaux, 1983.

Flew, Anthony. "Miracles." In *The Encyclopedia of Philosophy*, edited by Paul Edwards, vol. 5. New York: Macmillan, 1967.

Frame, Randy. "Dismissal: Three Professors Part Paths with Dallas." *Christianity Today*, 5 February 1988.

Freud, Sigmund. *The Future of an Illusion*. Revised and edited by James Strachey. Garden City, N.Y.: Doubleday, 1964.

Gardner, Martin. *Fads and Fallacies*. New York: Dover, 1974.

Geisler, Norman L. *The Creator in the Courtroom*. Grand Rapids: Baker Book House, 1982.

Geisler, Norman L., and J. Kerby Anderson. *Origin Science*. Grand Rapids: Baker, 1987.

Gilkey, Langdon. *Creationism on Trial: Evolution and God at Little Rock*. Minneapolis: Winston, 1985.

Hoyle, Fred, and N. C. Wickramasinghe. *Evolution from Space*. London: Dent, 1981.

Hume, David. *An Enquiry concerning Human Understanding*. 2nd ed. Oxford: Oxford University Press, 1902.

Jastrow, Robert. *God and the Astronomers*. New York: Norton, 1978.

———. "A Scientist Caught between Two Faiths." Interview by Bill Durbin. *Christianity Today*, 6 August 1982.

———. *Until the Sun Dies*. New York: Norton, 1977.

Koch, Kurt E. *Christian Counseling and Occultism*. Grand Rapids: Kregel, 1972.

———. *Occult Bondage and Deliverance*. Grand Rapids: Kregel, 1976.

Kole, Andre, and Al Janssen. *Miracles or Magic?* Eugene, Ore.: Harvest House, 1984.

Korem, Danny, and Paul Meier. *Powers: Testing the Psychic and Supernatural*. Downers Grove, Ill.: 1988.

Kusche, Lawrence D. *The Bermuda Triangle Mystery—Solved*. New York: Harper & Row, 1975.

———. *The Disappearance of Flight 19*. New York: Harper and Row, 1980.

Larue, Gerald A. *Free Inquiry* (Committee for the Scientific Examination of Religion), Fall 1986.

Lawson, Steven. "Faith Preacher Hobart Freeman Dies." *Charisma*, February 1985.

Lewis, C. S. *Miracles*. London: Bles, 1947.

————. *The Screwtape Letters*. New York: Macmillan, 1961.

Newton, Isaac. *Mathematical Principles of Natural Philosophy*. Vol. 34 of *Great Books of the Western World*. Chicago: Encyclopaedia Britannica, 1952.

Nolen, William A. *Healing: A Doctor in Search of a Miracle*. New York: Random House, 1974.

North, Gary. *None Dare Call It Witchcraft*. New Rochelle, N.Y.: Arlington House, 1976.

Parker, Larry. *We Let Our Son Die*. Irvine, Cal.: Harvest House, 1980.

Pelletier, Kenneth. *Christian Medical Society Journal* 11, No.1 (1980).

Peters, George W. *Indonesia Revival*. Grand Rapids: Zondervan, 1973.

Pike, James A. As quoted in *Time*, 28 June 1976.

Randi, James. *Flim-Flam*. Buffalo: Prometheus, 1982.

Robertson, Pat, with Bob Slosser. *The Secret Kingdom*. Toronto: Bantam, 1984.

Rogo, D. Scott. *Miracles: A Parascientific Inquiry into Wondrous Phenomena*. Chicago: Contemporary Books, Inc., 1983.

Rosen, Harold. *A Scientific Report on "The Search for Bridey Murphy."* New York: Julian, 1956.

Ruse, Michael. *Science Technology and Human Values*. Summer 1982.

Sagan, Carl. *Broca's Brain*. New York: Random House, 1979.

Sandage, Allan. "A Scientist Reflects on Religious Belief." *Truth: An International, Interdisciplinary Journal of Christian Thought* 1 (1985).

Sarles, Ken L. "An Appraisal of the Signs and Wonders Movement." *Bibliotheca Sacra* (January-March 1986):145:577:80.

Signs and Wonders Today. Ed. by the editors of *Christian Life* with the cooperation of C. Peter Wagner. Wheaton, Ill.: Christian Life, 1983.

Smith, Chuck. *Charisma vs. Charismania*. Eugene, Ore.: Harvest House, 1983.

Smith, George H. *Atheism: The Case against God*. Buffalo: Prometheus, 1979.

Smith, Joseph. "Pearl of Great Price." *Doctrine and Cov-*

enants. Salt Lake City: Church of Jesus Christ of the Latter-day Saints, 1974.

Spinoza, Benedict. *Tractatus Theologica-Politicus*. Vol. 1 of *The Chief Works of Benedict de Spinoza*. London: George Bell, 1883.

Stafford, Tim. "Testing the Wine from John Wimber's Vineyard." *Christianity Today*, 8 August 1986.

Sugue, Thomas. *The Story of Edgar Cayce: There Is a River*. Rev. ed. Virginia Beach: Association for Research and Enlightenment, 1973.

Tari, Mel. *Like a Mighty Wind*. Carol Stream, Ill.: Creation House, 1971.

Trefil, James S. "Closing in on Creation." *Smithsonian*, May 1983.

White, Mel. *Deceived*. Old Tappan, N.J.: Revell, 1979.

Wilkerson, David. *The Vision*. New York: Pillar Books, 1974.

Wimber, John, with Kevin Springer. *Power Evangelism*. San Francisco: Harper & Row, 1986.

———. *Power Healing*. San Francisco: Harper & Row, 1987.

Yockey, Hubert P. "Self Organization Origin of Life Scenarios and Information Theory." *Journal of Theoretical Biology* (1981).